"Jerry Bridges has lived the Christ-centered life that he's long taught and written about. I've personally benefited immensely from his writings on God's holiness and providence. Years ago I led a group of men in a rich study of his book *The Joy of Fearing God*. Having several meals and conversations with Jerry allowed me to witness firsthand a Jesus-exalting humility that has stayed with me as much as his writings. I thank God for Jerry Bridges and I am thrilled at the release of *God Took Me by the Hand*!"

RANDY ALCORN,
Eternal Perspective Ministries; bestselling author of *Heaven*

"I have benefited greatly from the writings of Jerry Bridges — and now I have benefited greatly from his life story. You will be thrilled by the working of providence in Jerry's life and reminded of how it is working, even now, in your own life."

STEVE FARRAR,
bestselling author of *Point Man* and *True Courage*

"Jerry Bridges is not new to me. But his story is. As I read through his book, one word kept recurring to me . . . *authentic*. If ever there was a time when this world needs to read, and hear, from men who are authentic, I believe that is now. As a matter of fact, those are the only books I have endeavored to read for the last eighteen years, and it has paid big dividends in my life and thinking. This book fits in that category."

RON DICIANNI,
award-winning painter; author

"Once again, Jerry Bridges gives us a modern day classic. In *God Took Me By the Hand* he paints a brilliant picture of the providence of God. In the most beautiful and personal way, Bridges weaves his life story through this compelling and definitive work on God's divine plan. Providence is this truth that God, in His supernatural way, nudges us toward His good and exhilarating plan for our lives. Bridges reminds that in spite of all the chaos, all our mistakes and shortcomings, He's got the whole world in His hands — even better — He's got your one and most important life in His hands."

PALMER CHINCHEN, PhD
pastor; author of *True Religion* and *The Barefoot Tribe*

GOD TOOK ME
by the HAND

A Story of God's
UNUSUAL PROVIDENCE

JERRY BRIDGES

A NavPress published resource in alliance
with Tyndale House Publishers, Inc.

NAVPRESS⬤

NavPress is the publishing ministry of The Navigators, an international Christian organization and leader in personal spiritual development. NavPress is committed to helping people grow spiritually and enjoy lives of meaning and hope through personal and group resources that are biblically rooted, culturally relevant, and highly practical.

For more information, visit www.NavPress.com.

© 2014 by Jerry Bridges

A NavPress published resource in alliance with Tyndale House Publishers, Inc.

ISBN 978-1-61291-579-1

Cover design by Gearbox
Cover image by iStock

Some of the anecdotal illustrations in this book are true to life and are included with the permission of the persons involved. All other illustrations are composites of real situations, and any resemblance to people living or dead is coincidental.

Unless otherwise identified, all Scripture quotations in this publication are taken from the Holy Bible, English Standard Version® (ESV®), copyright © 2001 by Crossway, a publishing ministry of Good News Publishers. ESV® Text Edition: 2011. Used by permission. All rights reserved. Other versions used include: the *Holy Bible, New International Version*® (NIV®). Copyright © 1973, 1978, 1984, 2011 by Biblica, Inc.® Used by permission of Zondervan. All rights reserved worldwide. www.zondervan.com The "NIV" and "New International Version" are trademarks registered in the United States Patent and Trademark Office by Biblica, Inc.®; and the King James Version (KJV).

Cataloging-in-Publication Data is Available.

Printed in the United States of America

19	18	17	16	15	14
6	5	4	3	2	1

To our grandchildren
Elise, Joseph, Joshua,
David, Brendan, Hannah, Sarah
With the prayer that in the course of time, each of you will
understand and appreciate the providence of God in your life.

Contents

Preface

The pages that follow were, in their original draft, intended to hopefully become a published book explaining and exalting the providence of God. But the more I worked on it, the more I sensed it was too personal to become a book, so I changed my mental audience to family and close friends. However, some folks at NavPress read my story and thought it could be useful to a larger audience, so here it is. Whether you know me or not, then, I pray that this book will be helpful to you to see how the providence of God can work in the life of a very ordinary individual.

I am indebted to Don Simpson, my longtime friend and editor, for his valuable help on the manuscript. I also want to thank Connie Trautman, my part-time administrative assistant, for her work in typing the manuscript, including the many changes I made over several months. And finally to Kris Wallen, a vice president at NavPress, for the continual encouragement and help she has been to me over the last few years.

CHAPTER 1

Introduction

D ecember 4, 2009, I celebrated my eightieth birthday. The year leading up to that was a time of questioning whether I would make an eightieth birthday. No one in my extended family on either side — aunts, uncles, cousins, or parents — had ever lived to be eighty. My older brother who I thought would break the "eighty barrier" died three weeks after his seventy-ninth birthday. But I did make it, and thanks to my family and my good friend Chris Thifault, it was a great celebration.

The year following, 2010, I did a lot of reflecting on God's working in my life for eighty years. As I reflected on His leading, this expression kept coming to my mind: "When I was seventeen years old, it seemed as if God took me by the hand and said, 'Come with Me.'" And for more than sixty-five years, God has, as it were, continued to hold my hand and lead me in the path He has marked out for me.

This does not mean that life has been a great success all these years. There have been lots of times when life has been hard and discouraging, but through it all, I see God's hand drawing me along the path He ordained for me before I was born. Because my growing up years were years of economic survival, I never dreamed big dreams nor aspired to do great things. All I wanted to do was make a decent living and be a good Christian. I had no idea what this would look like in the future. Humanly speaking, I certainly was not a candidate to be someone used by God as has happened.

The pages that follow are a record of the sixty-five-year journey of being led by God's hand. My personal story is not important except to illustrate the providence of God, what I call the invisible hand of God, in terms that twenty-first-century readers can understand. My perspective of present-day Christendom is that very few people have any understanding of the providence of God and so fail to appreciate God's continued care and action in their lives. For those unfamiliar with the expression "the providence of God," I will explain it in chapter 3.

The purpose of this story, then, is to explain, illustrate, and exalt God's providence. My life's story is meant to be only a backdrop and a series of illustrations of specific acts of the invisible hand of God so that many believers will come to recognize and appreciate more of God's work in their own lives.

CHAPTER 2

An Unpromising Beginning

The 500 block of Oakland Avenue ran parallel to and about ten yards west of the railroad tracks. Those ten yards between the tracks and the street were owned by the railroad company and sat empty most of the time. The one exception was when the railroad used that empty land to store rail ties.

Across the unpaved road, alone in the middle of the block, sat a small four-room house, 521 South Oakland Avenue. I do not know the origin of the house, but it quite possibly had been servants' quarters for the larger house on the other side of the block. Whatever its origin, the house was very plain. There were no closets. Clothes were hung on hooks on the walls. There were no kitchen cabinets. The house did have indoor plumbing, but there was no hot water heater. In order to wash clothes or the dishes or to take a bath, one had to heat water on the kitchen stove and mix it with cold water from the faucets. I was born in this house on December 4, 1929. My parents named me Gerald Dean but

13

called me Jerry, and that is the name I have gone by all my life, except in legal and financial documents.

My parents were Emmett and Lillian Bridges. Both had grown up on East Texas cotton farms, and both had dropped out of school after eighth grade to work on the farms. They were married about 1924, and Dad started raising cotton on rented land. Their first child was born June 4, 1926, and was named William Jackson but was called Jack. Sometime after Jack was born, my dad realized he could never succeed raising cotton on rented land, so he sold what little assets he had and moved the family to Tyler, Texas, a town of about twenty thousand people. His plan was to go to a business college and study accounting. However, he got sidetracked.

He took a job with a farm supply store which also had a cotton brokerage business. The owners of the company talked him into studying cotton grading so he could become their cotton buyer. The problem was that buying cotton was seasonal, and Dad spent the rest of the year as a clerk in the farm supply store. Humanly speaking, this was not a good decision. Though Dad had dropped out of school after eighth grade, he was very intelligent and was especially good in math. I'm sure he would have made an excellent basic accountant. However, viewed from the perspective I now have, I am confident God was sovereignly directing that seemingly bad decision. God is as much in control of our bad decisions as He is our good ones. This does not mean God *causes* us to make bad decisions any more than He causes us to sin. But He does allow us to sin, and He does allow us to make our bad decisions.

When I was born I had four physical defects. The first and most obvious was that I was cross-eyed. For those not familiar with this term, it means that while one eye looks straight ahead the other eye is turned toward the nose. The second and most difficult to deal with is that my right inner ear was not fully developed. As a young child I was not aware of my deafness in that ear, but I became increasingly aware of it and the accompanying inconvenience as I grew older. It was not until I was eighty-two that an ear, nose, and throat doctor discovered the cause of my deafness which I had had all my life.

The third and fourth defects were deformities in my breastbone and spine. Actually, these two were not significant in my growing up years, but both became quite a problem in adult life. Then to add insult to injury, I became left-handed in a right-handed world. I did not get off to a good start physically.

My parents were members of a "fundamentalist" church. That word did not have the derogatory ring in those days that it has now. Nevertheless, it was a small, separatist church. My mother was a homebody who never learned to drive and didn't socialize much in the neighborhood. In fact, her whole social life took place in the church. Dad worked from eight a.m. to six p.m. six days a week. With church activities on Sunday, he had no time for neighborhood socializing.

To sum it up, my parents were financially poor, education dropouts, and religiously and socially isolated. This was not a good beginning for me.

My brother, Jack, started school when I was only two years old, and there were no boys my age in the neighborhood, so I grew up alone until I started school at age six. We had no toys, so I played in my imagination. My favorite was pretending to be an over-the-road truck driver complete with all the sounds of engines revving up and gears meshing, which I heard in the real trucks in my neighborhood.

Finally the day came in 1936 for me to start school. Our school system did not have a kindergarten grade at that time, so I started in first grade. Again, because my mother was a homebody, instead of taking me to school the first day, she sent me with my brother, Jack, who was entering fifth grade. All was well until we got to the school, and then Jack did not know what to do with me. He was so bewildered he started to cry and the principal came along, asked his problem, and got me safely to my first grade class.

Years later, as I thought back on my early childhood from the advantage of knowing what I had learned about the providence of God, two verses of Scripture helped. They are Psalm 139:13 and 16: "For you formed my inward parts; you knitted me together in my mother's womb. . . . Your eyes saw my unformed substance; in your book were written, every one of them, the days that were formed for me, when as yet there was none of them."

First of all, I realized that God had created me to be physically the person He wanted me to be, birth defects and all. When I look at David's phrase, "you knitted me together in my mother's womb," I can think, "David, you did not know anything about genetics that we know today," but the truth is, the Holy Spirit, who guided David to write those words, knows infinitely more about genetics than the most brilliant scientists. So when He guides David to say, "You knitted me together in my mother's womb," He is saying that God so controlled the genetics that I became physically exactly the person He wanted me to be. The same is true about the fact that the days that were ordained for me, including those early difficult days, were written in His book before one of them came to be.

So I was born physically exactly the way God wanted me to be and to parents who were poor, uneducated, and socially isolated, all because that was the plan God ordained for me before I was born.

But if you fast-forward my life to the present, you have to be amazed at what God has done for a cross-eyed, partially deaf boy growing up in poverty alongside the railroad tracks. As I think of myself, I am continually reminded of the words of Psalm 40:1-3:

> I waited patiently for the LORD; he inclined to me and heard my cry. He drew me up from the pit of destruction, out of the miry bog, and set my feet upon a rock, making my steps secure. He put a new song in my mouth, a song of praise to our God. Many will see and fear, and put their trust in the LORD.

Though David's reference to the "pit of destruction" and the "miry bog" far overstates my situation, the idea of

17

God drawing me up and setting my feet upon a rock is exactly how I view God's work in my life.

Furthermore, all that God has done, He has done solely by His grace. Apart from Christ I deserve nothing but His eternal judgment. In fact I could easily appropriate the title of one of John Bunyan's works, *Grace Abounding to the Chief of Sinners*. And I readily identify with Jacob, who was himself an amazing illustration of God's grace, when he said, "I am not worthy of the least of all the deeds of steadfast love and all the faithfulness that you have shown to your servant, for with only my staff I crossed this Jordan, and now I have become two camps" (Genesis 32:10).

We will continue to pursue God's providential working in chapter 4, but I want to turn aside from my story now and in chapter 3 set the biblical foundation for everything that will transpire from this point onward. We are going to look at three truths that are necessary to understand biblically the events of my life and the lives of most Christians. These truths are:

- The providence of God
- The common grace of God
- The instruction and guidance of the Holy Spirit

CHAPTER 3

The Biblical Foundation

THE PROVIDENCE OF GOD

God's providence is His constant care for and His absolute rule over all His creation for His own glory and the good of His people. Note the absolute terms: *constant care, absolute rule, all creation.* Note also the two major divisions of His providence: His *care* for His creation and His *rule* over His creation. We are going to look at these in reverse order. So first of all, let's take apart the expression "His absolute rule over all His creation."

To say that God rules can give us an image of a king ruling from his throne, making major decisions but basically unaware of the day-to-day events occurring in his kingdom. But to say that God rules over His creation is to say that He controls all events and circumstances. Absolutely nothing can happen outside the controlling hand of God. Consider the following Scriptures which are only a sample of the many we could look at:

Who has spoken and it came to pass, unless the Lord has commanded it? (Lamentations 3:37)

Is it not from the mouth of the Most High that good and bad come? (Lamentations 3:38)

Are not two sparrows sold for a penny? And not one of them will fall to the ground apart from your Father. (Matthew 10:29)

Instead you ought to say, "If the Lord wills, we will live and do this or that." (James 4:15)

We all make plans, but those plans can succeed only when they are consistent with God's purpose. In the same manner, no one can thwart God's plans. As the mighty King Nebuchadnezzar said, "All the inhabitants of the earth are accounted as nothing, and he does according to his will among the host of heaven and among the inhabitants of the earth; and none can stay his hand or say to him, 'What have you done?'" (Daniel 4:35). This is what we mean when we say that God controls all the events and circumstances of His creation.

However, God not only controls all events and circumstances, He *directs* all of them so that they accomplish His purposes. God is "hands on" in directing the affairs of His creation. Note the references to God's acting in the following verses:

The king's heart is a stream of water in the hand of the LORD; he turns it wherever he will. (Proverbs 21:1)

The LORD stirred up the spirit of Cyrus king of Persia, so that he made a proclamation throughout all his kingdom and also put it in writing. (Ezra 1:1)

Thanks be to God, who put into the heart of Titus the same earnest care I have for you. (2 Corinthians 8:16)

God not only directs all things to accomplish His purposes, He *orchestrates* all diverse events, things we consider "good" and things we consider "bad," so that the end product displays the beauty of His glory. See, for example:

As for you, you meant evil against me, but God meant it for good, to bring it about that many people should be kept alive, as they are today. (Genesis 50:20)

And we know that for those who love God all things work together for good, for those who are called according to his purpose. (Romans 8:28)

So we see that the providence of God covers all events and circumstances in His creation. Oftentimes when we speak of the providence of God, we have in mind some unusual event, but the fact is all of life is lived under the providence of God. Suppose I drive to the grocery store, and on returning, I am spared in a rather unusual way from a life-shattering accident. I gladly speak then of the providence of God in sparing me. But suppose my drive home is uneventful. This too is under the providence of God.

There is an interesting little anecdote about Jesus recorded in Matthew 17:24-27 that I believe beautifully illustrates the providence of God. The temple tax collector asked Peter whether Jesus paid the tax. Without getting into all the story, Jesus told Peter, "Go to the sea and cast a hook and take the first fish that comes up, and when you open its mouth you will find a shekel. Take that and give it to them for me and for yourself."

The question we may ask is, was this a miracle or an act of God's providence? It could have been a miracle. If Jesus could turn water into wine and feed five thousand men plus women and children with two fish and five barley cakes, He certainly could create a coin in the mouth of a fish.

But suppose it was an act of God's providence. It might happen something like this: Someone *happened* to drop a shekel into the sea. A fish sees it and, thinking it is food, takes it into its mouth. The shekel is too large to swallow and remains stuck in the fish's mouth. Meanwhile Jesus tells Peter to cast his hook into the water and take the first fish that comes up. The fish with the coin just *happens* to be right where Peter casts his hook. Peter catches it, and lo and behold, there is a coin of the exact amount needed in the mouth of the fish.

Assuming this event was an act of God's providence, everything in the story, except for Jesus' knowledge that the fish would be right where Peter cast his hook, could be repeated today. But would not God have been just as much involved in guiding this series of seemingly insignificant events as He would have been in miraculously creating a coin in the mouth of the fish?

This is the way God's providence works. He is constantly ruling, directing, and orchestrating all events in His entire universe to accomplish His purposes. An expression has crept into our Christian lingo: "That was a God thing." Although the statement is intended to recognize the hand of God in the event, it unwittingly suggests God is not at work in the ordinary events of life. When we think like this, we fail to give God the glory that is due Him.

In the story that follows, you will see some examples of God's unusual providence in causing certain events to happen in my life. But these events are unusual, not only in their effect on my life but also in the fact that there are so few of them. I would say that despite the unusual occasions, most of my life has been lived under the ordinary providence of God, that is, the "unseen hand" of God ruling, directing, and orchestrating all of the ordinary events and circumstances of my life.

THE COMMON GRACE OF GOD

God's common grace is an expression of His constant care for all His creation. It may be simply defined as His temporal blessings given to all humanity, saved and unsaved alike. As Jesus said in Matthew 5:45, "For he makes his sun rise on the evil and on the good, and sends rain on the just and on the unjust."

The public school I attended in Tyler and the university where I went were good schools. With rare exception I had good or even excellent teachers and received a good education. But so did the unbelieving students who were in the same classes. The teachers and professors may or may not have been believers, but God used all of them to provide my education. That is God's common grace.

The same is true in all areas of life. My cardiology doctor is a good doctor who may or may not be a Christian, and I receive good care. But so do all the doctor's patients who may or may not be believers. Illustrations such as this could be cited hundreds of times. Most of life is lived under God's common grace. This applies equally to believers and unbelievers.

Obviously, the sin of Adam, and the resulting curse by God on creation, have to some degree marred the expression of God's common grace and also caused it to have differing effects on each of us. As God says in Amos 4:7, "I also withheld the rain from you when there were yet three months to the harvest; I would send rain on one city, and send no rain on another city; one field would have rain, and the field on which it did not rain would wither." We had a massive forest fire at the western edge of our city in 2012. The fire consumed 346 houses in just one neighborhood while the adjacent neighborhoods on either side were spared. God's common grace is not evenly dispersed.

One of the unrecognized expressions of common grace is that God teaches us knowledge. Psalm 94:10 says,

"He who teaches man knowledge." Isaiah 28:24-29, written in the context of an agricultural setting, is a beautiful example of this.

> Does he who plows for sowing plow continually?
>> Does he continually open and harrow his
>> ground?
> When he has leveled its surface,
>> does he not scatter dill, sow cumin,
> and put in wheat in rows
>> and barley in its proper place,
>> and emmer as the border?
> For he is rightly instructed;
>> his God teaches him.
>
> Dill is not threshed with a threshing sledge,
>> nor is a cart wheel rolled over cumin,
> but dill is beaten out with a stick,
>> and cumin with a rod.
> Does one crush grain for bread?
>> No, he does not thresh it forever;
> when he drives his cart wheel over it
>> with his horses, he does not crush it.
> This also comes from the LORD of hosts;
>> he is wonderful in counsel
>> and excellent in wisdom.

Note how the practical wisdom of the farmer is attributed to God who teaches him. Today we have what seems to be an explosion of knowledge coming from research universities and hospitals. Think of all the advances in medical treatment that have occurred in the last forty to fifty years, or all that has occurred in space travel and exploration. This knowledge comes from God as an expression of His common grace.

Meanwhile, what about the ordinary expressions of common grace? The farmer who was taught practical wisdom as depicted in Isaiah 28 still has to be taught today. Yes, he may go to the state agricultural school and learn the latest techniques and methods that will make him a better farmer, but where did that advanced knowledge ultimately come from? All knowledge and wisdom ultimately comes from God who guides the research of scientists and inventors in their various quests and who gives practical wisdom to the farmer or business sense to those in business.

The knowledge that enabled Alexander Graham Bell to invent the first telephone and Thomas Edison to invent the first lightbulb in the nineteenth century, as well as the development of digital communication and the mapping of human DNA in our day, all came from God. Every temporal blessing that we enjoy is ultimately an expression of God's common grace.

I am making a point of this because I believe even we who are believers take God's common grace for granted. We expect our gas furnace to start on a cold winter morning, or the air conditioner to kick in on a hot, sultry day. We expect the food we want to buy to be on the supermarket shelf ready for us to pick up. We get upset when the furnace doesn't come on, or annoyed when a particular food item we expected to buy is not there, but are we thankful when the furnace does come on and the grocery item is on the shelf? When the apostle Paul said to "[give] thanks *always* and for *everything*" (Ephesians 5:20, emphasis added), he was not thinking only of our spiritual blessings. He was including all our temporal blessings, all the expressions of God's common grace, as well.

As we go through my journey, we will see instances of what I call unusual acts of providence. But these are the exceptions. The vast majority of my life has been lived within the ordinary arena of God's common grace. And I suspect yours has been also.

THE INSTRUCTION AND GUIDANCE OF THE HOLY SPIRIT

The words of Scripture are unique in that they are breathed out by God (see 2 Timothy 3:16). How are we to understand the expression "breathed out"? It means that the writers of Scripture were "carried along" or that their thought processes were so infallibly guided by the Holy Spirit that they wrote exactly what He wanted them to write (see 2 Peter 1:21). Thus we can confidently say that what Scripture says, God says.

By contrast, all of us who teach the Word of God, whether by speech or by writing, prayerfully depend on (or at least should depend on) the Holy Spirit to guide us in our preparation and delivery (or writing). But we do not expect

His guidance to be infallibly received by us. No evangelical commentator, for example, believes that the words of his commentary carry the same authority as Scripture.

So when we speak of the Holy Spirit's instruction and guidance of us today, we should keep in mind that what we perceive to be His instruction and guidance is not infallible. It is not that the Holy Spirit does not speak infallibly but that He has not so operated on our minds that we receive it infallibly.

There are times when many of us believe that the Holy Spirit has guided us, whether in increased understanding of Scripture or in some course of action. But we do not believe that our perception or understanding of His guidance is infallible. Therefore, any perceived instruction or guidance of the Holy Spirit is always subject to and must be tested by the infallible authority of Scripture.

But the question arises, how does the Holy Spirit instruct and guide us? The primary means, of course, is through His authoritative Scriptures. That word may come to us through our own reading or study of Scriptures or through the teaching or writing ministry of those God has gifted for these roles. I myself have received instruction or guidance through all of these means, but I do not regard my own conclusions from Bible reading or study, or the words of another teacher or writer, to be infallible. So the Scriptures are infallible and inerrant, but our understanding of them is not. Rather, it is often conditioned by our previous understanding or biases.

The Spirit may also instruct or guide us in particular

situations through direct impressions on our minds. These impressions may be a strong sense of urging that I should do something or a strong sense of restraint that I should not do something. But our understanding of these impressions is not infallible. I can think of one occasion when I thought I had an impression from God, but subsequent events did not bear that out. Therefore, we should treat impressions with caution, and above all, make sure they are in accordance with the truths of Scripture.

A third way the Holy Spirit instructs or guides us is through precise words planted in our minds, so precise that it seems as if another person is speaking to us. I call this the "inaudible voice" of the Holy Spirit. I know this way is controversial, and many people whom I respect are adamant that the Holy Spirit never communicates this way. Their objection is that such phenomena would be equated to divine revelation on a par with Scripture. But divine revelation by definition adds new content by which God reveals truths for the whole church. With the closing of the canon of Scripture, we believe such revelation no longer occurs.

What I am saying is that the Holy Spirit sometimes speaks to us in that inaudible voice by way of illumination or application of Scripture to one's personal life. One important caution we should exercise is to recognize that we are not infallible receptors of the Holy Spirit's words. Thus the "inaudible voice" of the Holy Spirit that we believe we have heard must again be tested against Scripture. The Holy Spirit will never "speak" to us in ways that are not in accordance with His Word.

You may wonder why I go into this subject so extensively. It is because I believe that the Spirit's interaction with our human spirits or our minds is part of His providential working in our lives. In my own life there have been perhaps eight or ten times over sixty-plus years when I believe the Holy Spirit has moved me in a certain direction either by a strong impression or through His "inaudible" voice. You cannot understand key incidents in my spiritual journey without knowing my position on this subject, whether you agree with it or not.

I was once challenged to prove from Scripture that the Holy Spirit does speak through the "inaudible voice." I replied that I cannot do that, but the person who believes He does not speak in this manner cannot prove his position from Scripture either. So how do we determine which view is correct? I believe the validity of these experiences can be determined by two tests. First and most important, of course, is whether it aligns with the objective teaching of Scripture. The second is, does it stand the test of time? That is, do subsequent events or actions you have taken as a result of an impression or an inaudible communication produce positive and God-honoring results? If these impressions or inaudible voice communications pass these tests, then I believe they are authentic workings of the Holy Spirit in our lives.

If you continue reading this book (and I realize that some who are so strongly opposed to my position may not continue), you will see illustrations of both strong impressions and the hearing of the inaudible voice. All these are important incidents, significant turning points in my journey with God.

Now let's continue with the story of God's unusual providence.

CHAPTER 4

School Days

The elementary school I attended served the section of the city where the wealthy lived all the way down to blue-collar families and some at the bottom of the scale like mine. I was probably the poorest of the poor.

Nevertheless, elementary school was a good experience for me. No one teased me about being cross-eyed or wearing hand-me-down clothes. I think first graders, at least at that time, were not conscious of financial or social distinctions and were friendly to all. I was a fairly good student, and my teachers accepted me on that basis.

There were a few hard experiences. First of all, when I was in third grade my teacher sent a note home to my parents saying that they should have my hearing tested. The problem was that my parents had no money except for the most urgent medical needs, so the testing was never done.

A second hard situation occurred every day at lunchtime. Our school had a hot lunch cafeteria, and each item cost five cents. Meat was five cents, potatoes were five cents, a half pint of milk was five cents, and so on. Most of the kids were given twenty-five cents to buy their lunch. I was given ten cents. Every day I had whatever meat was on the menu and mashed potatoes, nothing more.

A third hard situation was also due to lack of money. From time to time our school had special programs in the auditorium, such as a magician or something like that. They always cost twenty-five cents. I was never given anything for those special programs, so I spent the time in my homeroom when all of my classmates went to the program.

The last significant hurt occurred at recess. The boys would always choose up sides to play football or baseball. Cross-eyed people have little or no depth perception because it is the two eyes focusing on the same object that produces depth perception. Because of my eyesight, I had almost no depth perception, so I could not tell where the ball was or how fast it was coming. Consequently, I would always be chosen last. When I was sixteen my parents finally had me get an operation to straighten my eyes. Cosmetically it worked, but by this time my eyes would not work together, so I still have the depth perception problem, primarily in driving.

But in spite of these hard situations, I enjoyed elementary school. I was conscientious, and I experienced the common grace of good teachers.

For some reason, when I started school our school system only had eleven grades. At the end of my fifth-grade year, they decided to move to a twelve-grade system. The way they accomplished this was to move every class from sixth grade up one year. That is, eleventh-grade seniors became twelfth-grade seniors, and so on. They made a break between sixth and fifth grades. Half of my fifth-grade class became seventh graders and the remainder became sixth graders. I think the division was based on age, with the older pupils becoming seventh graders and the younger ones going into sixth grade. Because my birthday is in December, I made the seventh-grade class.

The immediate result of moving up the classes was that the students were graduating a year younger. My brother graduated as a twelfth grader when he was sixteen, although he was soon to be seventeen. Later, I graduated at the age of seventeen and did not turn eighteen until December of my freshman year in college.

Because I was a good student, I enjoyed junior high (now called middle school). Ninth-grade boys could go out for a junior high football team. As a ninth grader, I stood five feet nine and weighed 142 pounds. I was one of the bigger boys in the class, so I made the team. Unfortunately, I stopped growing. When I finally graduated from high school, I was still at five feet nine and had grown to 154 pounds (more about that later).

During junior high days I had a morning paper route which covered the central business district of town. I got up at four a.m., picked up my papers, delivered them, and was home in bed by six a.m. I slept until seven a.m. before getting up to go to school. I also worked Saturdays at a Safeway store from seven a.m. to seven p.m. I was paid three dollars for twelve hours of work.

For the first time I had my own discretionary income. The first thing I bought was a refurbished bicycle. This was during World War II, and no new bicycles (or anything else) were being produced. I think every manufacturing plant that could be converted was producing material for the military.

A downside from my junior high years was ninth-grade algebra. I took that in the school year of 1943–1944, right at the height of World War II. The normal algebra teacher, who was very good, was away with her husband at some army post. Her substitute was a young woman fresh out of college with a degree in English. As a result, I was not well-grounded in the fundamentals of algebra. This haunted me all the way through engineering school.

Here again, however, in hindsight, I can now see the Lord's invisible hand in that situation. Because I realized at the end of my freshman year in college that I did not have a good foundation in algebra, I changed my major from electrical engineering, which involves a great deal of math, to a curriculum called general engineering, a hybrid degree combining the basics of civil, electrical, and mechanical engineering with the fundamental courses in business administration. I later found those courses more useful to me than the engineering subjects. So again, God was at work providentially directing the change in my degree to something that would be more useful in His service.

A traumatic event of my ninth-grade experience was the death of my mother at age forty-one on February 7, 1944. I had just turned fourteen years old only two months before. Mother had been ill for about three weeks, but again, because of a shortage of finances, she never received a doctor's care. Just at the time when Dad and I thought she was getting better, she died suddenly one night. My brother had already graduated from high school and was studying for the ministry at a Bible institute in Fort Worth, so Dad and I were home alone.

After the funeral Jack returned to school, and Dad received lots of support from the other adults in our church. I received none. I went back to my ninth-grade classes, and none of my teachers or fellow students said anything to me about the death of my mother. I was all alone in my grief, but as the British would say, "I kept a stiff upper lip." In fact, I did not even cry until six months after her death.

My dad remarried in the fall of that year to a lady who had been a casual friend of the family for some years. At the time of their marriage, Dad and I finally moved from the little four-room house without hot water to a duplex owned by my stepmother's father.

I continued to play football, though this was probably a mistake. The other boys were continuing to grow while I remained static. By our senior year I was one of the smallest boys on the team. It's okay to be small if one is quick or fast, but I was neither, so I got very little playing time in my senior year. Looking back I can see that I should have dropped football after the tenth grade, because I had neither the size nor the athletic skills to continue. I believe that the sovereignty of God allows for us to make mistakes, at least from a human point of view, but there are no mistakes with God. What His purpose was in allowing me to make that mistake I do not know. As Deuteronomy 29:29 says,

"The secret things belong to the LORD our God."

I was a good student in high school, was selected for the National Honor Society, and graduated probably in the lower part of the top 10 percent of the graduates.

Meanwhile, during my growing-up years, our little fundamentalist church had grown rapidly. The church was renamed Central Baptist Church to distance itself from the fundamentalist environment. As was true of all Baptist churches in the South at that time, our church had an altar call every Sunday morning and evening. Our pastor was more of an evangelist than a pastor, so he placed a lot of emphasis on the altar call. When I was nine years old someone asked me, "When are you going to go forward and get saved?" I thought to myself, "I suppose now is the time." So the next Sunday evening I went forward. Our pastor must have thought that the very act of going forward was the act of trusting Christ as Savior, so no one prayed with me or went through the gospel with me. But I thought I was saved.

Two years later, during the altar call, for some reason I had real doubt about whether I was actually saved, so I went forward again. The same thing happened at that time. No one reviewed the gospel for me or invited me to pray to ask Christ to be my Savior.

I know the next thing sounds weird, and probably only people from Baptist churches in the South can understand this, but at age thirteen the same thing happened. This time, however, when I went home I looked at myself in the mirror and said, "You know that nothing happened to you tonight, but you are not going forward again." So I spent the next five years trying to convince myself that I must be a Christian because I did not want to go forward again during another altar call. This issue was finally resolved when I was eighteen years of age, but we will get to that later.

One obvious lesson to draw from this is that simply responding to an altar call or praying the "sinner's prayer" does not necessarily mean that one is born again. As Jesus said about the work of the Holy Spirit in John 3:7-8, "Do not marvel that I said to you, 'You must be born again.' The wind blows where it wishes, and you hear its sound, but you do not know where it comes from or where it goes. So it is with everyone who is born of the Spirit." We do need to understand and believe the gospel, and we do need to place our trust in Jesus as our Lord and Savior; but in the final result, it is the sovereign work of the Holy Spirit that makes us new creations in Christ.

As I look back on my public school days, there were no unusual evidences of God's providence in my life until my senior year. Despite some hard times, especially the death of my mother when I was fourteen, life was pretty ordinary. But that does not mean God was not active. I was living within the realm of His common grace. I was not yet a genuine born-again Christian, though I tried to convince myself that I was, and I'm sure the people in our church thought I was. But the truth is, you can do all the right things and believe the right doctrine and still not be a genuine believer. But God was going to take care of that.

CHAPTER 5

A New Beginning

There are two Old Testament stories that intrigue me
because they illustrate the providence of God directing
the events of ordinary people's lives. The first is the story of
Ruth, the Moabite widow and daughter-in-law of Naomi
from Bethlehem. One day after their return from the land of
Moab, Ruth asked permission to glean in the field of whoever
granted her favor.

So she set out to glean and the text says, "she happened
to come to the part of the field belonging to Boaz" (Ruth
2:3). Note the word *happened*, an expression we usually
associate with unplanned chance events. But God through
His providence led Ruth to Boaz's field. This was no
chance event. Ruth married Boaz and ultimately became
the great-grandmother of David. Ruth's happening to end
up in the field of Boaz was directed by the unseen hand of
God.

A similar event occurred in the story of Esther. One
night when the fate of the entire Jewish nation was on the
line, Ahasuerus, king of the Medo-Persian Empire, could
not sleep, so he gave orders to bring the book of the

memorable deeds of the kingdom to be read before him. Though the text does not state this, it seems that the reader just *happened* to read the account of how Mordecai had earlier saved the king from an assassination plot. Without going into all that happened before and after that night, suffice it to say that was the turning point for the salvation of the Jewish nation. All because the reader of the memorable deeds just *happened* to read in the section where Mordecai had saved the life of the king.

Both of these stories have special meaning for me because a small event that turned out to be a life-changing event just *happened* to me in my last semester of high school. As I began that last semester of my senior year, the future was a blank. I wanted to go to college but had never worked out a plan for doing it. My father, of course, was in no position to advise me or help pay for college expenses. Our high school had no guidance counselor to help us find scholarships or anything like that. Student loans were not available until years later. In short, I had no plans and no money. We did have a small junior college (now called community colleges) that shared our high school campus, but I had not even investigated what they had to offer.

Along about February, one night I was browsing through our local evening newspaper. Buried somewhere in the middle of the paper was a one-column article no more than four inches long that I just *happened* to see. The article was announcing a new program by the US Navy to train more officers by sending them to state universities, paying for their education, giving them some basic naval training, and granting them a commission as an officer in the navy upon graduation. The article closed by advising anyone interested to contact the nearest navy recruiting office.

I was at their office the next afternoon. I applied to take the entrance exam, which was a four-hour exam consisting of eight thirty-minute sections. The exam was designed so that no one would finish any of the eight sections. That way they got a true ranking of the examinees. I walked out of the exam thinking, *well, so much for that,* because I had never before taken an exam that you were not expected to finish. Much to my surprise, I made the cut and was accepted into the program, pending the passing of a physical examination. Along with the letter of acceptance was a medical history to be filled out and taken to the physical examination. It had not occurred to me until I was filling out that history that my hearing loss could disqualify me. I had no idea of the extent of my loss, so I put down "slight hearing loss in right ear."

I was directed to go to the Dallas Naval Station for the physical exam. For some reason they did not test my hearing. At the conclusion of the exam, the commanding officer of the medical unit looked over my paperwork to make sure all was in order. When he saw my notation about a slight hearing loss he asked me, "How did you do on your hearing test today?" I replied, "Sir, they did not give me one." He sat up in his chair and said, "They didn't give you one? Come with me." We walked out into the hallway. He said, "Stand here and put your left hand over your ear." He walked about twenty paces away and said, "Repeat after me." He started whispering numbers. I could repeat them after him so he walked back into his office, pulled a new medical history form out of his desk, and said, "Sit down. Fill out this form again. You have no hearing loss." This was an amazing act of God's providence. Remember from chapter 2 that, though I did not know it at the time, I did not have a "slight hearing loss." Rather, I was totally deaf in my right ear, yet I passed the hearing test.

A few weeks later I received a list of schools where the navy had a contract for this new program. We were told we could go to any school that we could get admitted to. I looked over the list and there were only two in Texas — Rice Institute (now Rice University) in Houston and the University of Texas in Austin. I didn't think I could make it through Rice, and I did not want to go to the University of Texas. The next closest school was the University of Oklahoma, so I put that down as my first choice and that is where I ended up going. So the high school boy who had no plans and no money suddenly found himself going to the University of Oklahoma, courtesy of the US Navy.

Let's back up and consider these circumstances. What are the chances of a high school boy browsing through the middle of a local paper and in particular spotting the article about the navy's new program? What were my chances of making the cut on the exam? What caused the medical officer at the Dallas Naval Air Station to give me a superficial hearing test and say to me, "You have no hearing problem"? All of this had to be God's handiwork, not only providing me with a college education but doing so in such a way that

I ended up in the navy. The significance of that fact will come out later.

When I wrote in chapter 1, "When I was seventeen years old, it seemed as if God took me by the hand and said, 'Come with me,'" the reading of that article in our daily paper was what I had in mind. That seemingly "chance" event, but in actuality, a providentially directed event, literally opened up for me all that has transpired since then.

Amazing, isn't it, that the infinite God who created the entire universe merely by His spoken word would condescend to intervene in the life of a cross-eyed, half-deaf young man and open up to him a future he could never have dreamed of. But this is the way God often works. He sometimes chooses the weak and lowly to accomplish His purposes so that He may be glorified in their weakness (see 1 Corinthians 1:27-29).

CHAPTER 6

College Days

I arrived at the train station in Norman, Oklahoma, at about five a.m. with most of my earthly possessions in two bags. I asked someone for directions to the university and started out with a bag in each hand. I had been assigned space in a temporary dormitory that was more than a mile from the train station. When I think today of walking that distance with a bag in each hand, it astonishes me. I do not remember having that much strength. Maybe those four years of football practice paid off after all.

The temporary dormitory was actually a former navy barracks without individual rooms. Several of us took the moveable closets and made a wall of them so that we had something of a room. One of my "roommates" just *happened* to be from Tyler. He had attended a military junior college for two years but had decided to take advantage of the navy program. I had never met John Bierman before because he was two years ahead of me in high school, but as fellow Tylerites we became good friends and roomed together for the next three-and-a-half years.

Since I was a good church kid, I joined First Baptist

Church right away and became involved in its student activities. Keep in mind, I was not yet a Christian, though I wanted to be and tried to act like one.

What the army and air force call cadets the navy calls midshipmen, a carryover from the British Navy several centuries ago when future officers were trained on the job aboard ship and were called midshipmen. I did well in school, but there was another midshipman who was much better academically than I. He dropped out of the program before the end of the first year, so for four years in a row I received the award for the outstanding academic midshipman of the year.

Each summer we had to go to sea or equivalent for practical training. Between my freshman and sophomore years our class was assigned to a heavy cruiser operating out of Norfolk, Virginia. We went all the way to Lisbon, Portugal, the British base at Gibraltar, and finally to Genoa, Italy. For an east Texas kid who had been out of state twice, once to Oklahoma and once to Louisiana, that was quite a trip.

We returned the middle of August, and I had two weeks at home before going back to school. During that time, my brother, who by that time was the assistant pastor at our church, called me one evening and asked if I would like to go with him to make a call. I was happy to go just to spend time with him. He called on one man who lacked assurance of salvation. In the course of the visit, my brother said to him, "If you don't know you are saved, you probably are not, because when you are saved you know it."

Today I would not make that statement so absolute,

but it was just what I needed to hear. After my brother dropped me off at Dad's house, I went to bed but I could not go to sleep. I finally faced the fact that I was not a Christian, so I prayed this prayer:

God, I don't know if I need to go forward again in church or not. I don't want to, but if I have to I am willing to. Whatever it takes, I want Jesus to be my Savior.

Immediately I had assurance of salvation and have not had any doubts about it since. I quickly went to sleep and had a good night's sleep. Later on I found Romans 5:1, which I thought described my experience: "Therefore, since we have been justified by faith, we have peace with God through our Lord Jesus Christ." That event occurred on a Thursday night before I returned to the university over the weekend.

That first week of classes, I was sitting at my desk in my dorm room one evening, getting ready to do an assignment. As I reached for the textbook for the class, I saw the small Bible that my dad had given to me when I was a senior in high school. I had had it for well over a year and had never opened it except at church on Sunday. As I saw the Bible, these words, clear as crystal, came into my mind: "Now that you really are a Christian, you need to start reading the Bible." I accepted those words as the voice of God because there was nothing in my background that would have triggered such a thought. Our pastor in Tyler, for example, never encouraged personal Bible reading. His attitude was that people grow by coming to church and hearing him preach. In any event, I received those words as the voice of God and began to read the Bible that night. I am still doing it sixty-four years later.

My sophomore year was fairly uneventful. I became interested in a lovely young lady at church, but that interest did not last too long. In hindsight, I can see that God was keeping me from a romantic relationship until it was time for the one He had for me.

At the beginning of my junior year, a public school classmate of mine, Bill McKensie, transferred to Oklahoma University from another school. During his first two years at the other school, he had been discipled by a Young Life staff member, and he began to pass on to me some of the basic things he was learning. We didn't spend a lot of time together, but just having him there was a great encouragement to me. This friendship in college turned out to have long-range consequences. Bill and his family eventually founded Pine Cove Conferences near Tyler. Because of my friendship with Bill, I became a frequent speaker at their family conferences.

Each year the navy would send a medical detachment to the university to give us a physical exam to make sure we were still qualified to remain in the program. Each year I passed a rather superficial hearing test. My junior year passed, again without significant events. Between my junior and senior years, however, we were to go on another cruise, this time as junior officers. We were to be trained to stand officer of the deck watches and in other responsibilities that we would assume one year later.

I was assigned to a destroyer sailing out of San Diego, California. We had been at sea only about a week when the North Korean army invaded South Korea. Immediately all military units on the West Coast and in the Far East were put on a war alert. This meant that all of the ships with midshipmen had to return to port and disembark us before heading to the Far East. Since all of this was so sudden, the navy had no plan B for training us for the summer. We ended up at the San Diego Naval Base going through various practical training courses, such as firefighting.

When I was in high school, our family listened to a Christian radio program called The Old Fashioned Revival Hour. The speaker was Charles E. Fuller, who later founded Fuller Theological Seminary. I never paid any attention to Dr. Fuller's sermons, but I enjoyed the music. In each program they always announced they were broadcasting from the Municipal Auditorium in Long Beach, California.

During one of my weekends at the San Diego Naval Base I decided to go to Long Beach and attend a live broadcast of The Old Fashioned Revival Hour. Dr. Fuller had always been interested in military people, and so each Sunday afternoon the first two rows of the middle section of the auditorium were reserved for men and women in uniform. As it turned out, there *happened* to be only two of us sitting in that section that day. At some point, the other person, a sailor, turned to me and said, "Have you ever memorized Scripture?" I responded, "I guess I have tried and I can quote a few verses like John 3:16." He said, "Write to The Navigators and ask them to send you the Topical

Memory System." He gave me their address.

When I returned to school in September I did write to The Navigators and began to go through the Topical Memory System, which at that time consisted of 108 verses. I worked through those 108 verses during my senior year, but when I finished I said, "Well, that is that." I put the verses away in my dresser drawer. The idea of continuing to review the verses and adding new verses somehow slipped right by me. But God was not through with me yet. Other than the Topical Memory System, I knew nothing about The Navigators. But through the TMS, as it was called, God was gradually introducing me to the organization I would be serving with for more than fifty-five years.

As a senior in college it is common to get interviews with companies interested in hiring new graduates. Even though I knew I had two years of obligated service in the navy to repay the government for my education, I decided to go for an interview just to get the experience. I ended up being invited to the offices of Southwestern Bell Telephone Company, one of the old "baby bells" of the AT&T conglomerate. Much to my surprise, they offered me a guaranteed job after I finished my two years of service. I would start in a management training program, which is exactly what my degree had prepared me for.

This seemed like an easy decision, but for some reason I decided not to accept their offer, so I graduated from OU leaving behind the prospects of marriage to a lovely young lady and a guaranteed job at Southwestern Bell. Why did I make these two choices? Both of them were made of my own volition without any sense of impression one way or the other from God, and I certainly did not pray about either of them. Nevertheless, God was as much at work in those decisions as in some of the later ones I will recount in this memoir.

When we speak of the sovereign will of God over the lives of people, some get the impression that we are making people puppets on the strings of God's sovereign will. The fact is, though, God works in our wills to cause us to do what He wants us to do, but He works in such a way that we do it voluntarily of our own free will.

This is different from the way we interact with one another. We can appeal, coerce, and manipulate to get another person to do what we want them to do. God does not work this way. He simply works within our will so that we make the choice ourselves, but we make the choice God wants us to make.

I referred in chapter 3 to Ezra 1:1, where we read that "the LORD stirred up the spirit of Cyrus king of Persia, so that he made a proclamation" regarding the return of the exiled Jews to their homeland. Cyrus did this of his own free will. In fact, he had never even heard of God (see Isaiah 45:4), but he did exactly what God wanted him to do. God often works this way in our lives today, and He certainly did in mine.

CHAPTER 7

Naval Service

June 4, 1951, I received my degree in general engineering from The University of Oklahoma and on the same evening was commissioned as an Ensign in the US Navy. I was assigned to an amphibious troop transport already operating in the Far East. The mission of an amphibious troop transport is to put soldiers or marines on the beach in an amphibious landing, such as was made famous at Normandy, France, on June 6, 1944.

I was sent first to amphibious assault training on the beaches of Coronado, California, and then on to Japan to catch up with the ship in Sasebo, Japan. Immediately I was assigned to begin standing junior officer of the deck watches. The officer of the deck is responsible for "driving" the ship when it is underway. He does this, of course, through commands to the helmsman and the engineers in the engine room below. I was also assigned to lead a wave of six small assault boats, each carrying thirty-two men from the ship to the beach. Actually, the only amphibious operation during the Korean War occurred before I got out there, so my activities were confined to training operations.

When our ship would go into a port, such as Hong Kong, I could see that most of the officers whom I had come to respect had a double moral standard. They did things overseas that they would never do at a port in the United States. At the same time, I had no defense against that activity. Fortunately, God kept me from getting involved, but I soon realized that I did not have the spiritual stamina to live a Christian life in such an ungodly atmosphere.

Since my ship had already been deployed to the Far East for some months before I went aboard, we returned to the United States after I was aboard only four months. Knowing that I needed some spiritual help, I sought out a Saturday night meeting in San Diego. In the States, when we went ashore, we usually put on civilian clothes, but at that Saturday night meeting there was one officer in uniform. I could easily spot him.

I said to myself, "He's either looking for something like I am or he's got it." After the meeting I managed to make my way toward him and introduce myself. He had just come in contact with The Navigators about six months before, and he was very zealous to pass on what he was learning. That night he gave me five or six disciplines that I should practice. These included such things as a daily quiet time, regular Bible reading and study, Scripture memorization, and personal evangelism. But it was like pouring water on concrete. I did not have enough maturity to even follow what he was saying, let alone make application to my own life.

We parted that night, and one would think that was the end of the story as far as my connection with The Navigators.

But God had other plans. The very next week his ship sent him to a three-day sonar seminar, and my ship sent me to a three-day radar seminar. We *happened* to be in adjacent classrooms and so met again in the hallway between sessions.

Jim said to me, "Would you like to go to a Navigators' Bible study with me tonight?" It turned out to be not a Navigators' study but more of a community study led by a Navigator staff member. The next day Jim said to me, "Would you like to go to a study at the Navigator's home?" I did not know what that meant, but I decided to go. He himself could not go, but he gave me directions, so I went to my first Navigators' Bible study in a Navigator's home.

To use a modern expression, "I was blown away." About half of the men in the room were World War II veterans who had been discipled by Navigator men during that time and who had been recalled to active duty for the Korean War. In my eyes, they were spiritual giants. They obviously knew the Lord in a way I had never dreamed of. I immediately decided that I wanted to be around these men and so began to attend the regular Friday night meeting. I also sent home for my Topical Memory System verse cards tucked away in a dresser drawer and began to review my Scripture memory program.

Soon I was invited to join a Navigators' Bible study meeting in a downtown church. One night the leader said to us, "The Bible was not given to increase your knowledge but to guide your conduct." That was not a good statement. The Bible is not a book of morals. Its main message is God's redemptive plan through Jesus Christ. It's true that biblical morals are a part of our salvation, but that's not where the emphasis should be.

Nevertheless, God used that statement in my mind, because the thought of applying the Bible to my daily life had never occurred to me. That night, on my way back to my ship, I prayed, "God, starting tonight, would You use the Bible to guide my conduct?" I think the seed of what would ultimately become my first book, *The Pursuit of Holiness*, was planted in my heart that night.

At that time, The Navigators used a series of question-and-answer Bible studies by Keith L. Brooks. They were simple, fill-in-the-blank type questions, but you had to look up in the Bible each of the verses used, so I began to see directly from Scripture that though conduct is not the main message of the Bible, the Bible certainly addresses it.

In God's plan for me, I never had the opportunity to be discipled by a Navigator staff over an extended period of time. After a couple of months in San Diego, my ship was sent to Bremerton, Washington Naval Shipyard for extended repairs and overhaul. I had been given the name and address of the Navigator staff member across Puget Sound in Seattle, but before I had a chance to get to know him, I received orders to another ship back in San Diego that was leaving immediately for the Far East.

The ship was an LST (landing ship, tank). The ship's mission was to land tanks and other vehicles on the beach in an amphibious landing operation. The ship had a crew of six officers and ninety enlisted men. There was a commanding officer, executive officer, and four division heads.

I was put in charge of the deck division, which had the responsibility for ship handling coming into or leaving port, standing watches while underway, and especially landing tanks at the beach.

I was in over my head from day one. Fortunately I had a veteran chief petty officer (the navy's equivalent of a master sergeant) who was skilled in all the various duties of our division, so I left all the technical details to him. The four division officers stood officer of the deck watches when we were underway. I served two four-hour watches each day, one in the daytime and one at night. I was no longer in training. I had major responsibilities.

We departed San Diego the day after I reported aboard when I hardly knew my way around the ship. We stopped at Pearl Harbor, then went south to Guam, then to Sasebo on Japan's west coast, and finally to our destination, the Yokosuka Naval Base on the south end of Tokyo Bay. This base was "home away from home" for most ships supporting the Korean War. I knew that The Navigators had sent a staff man to Yokosuka to minister to navy and marine personnel. I immediately contacted him and wanted to be discipled by him, but he was soon sent by The Navigators to Okinawa. He was replaced by two men sent to take his place.

We spent most of 1952 and the early part of 1953 conducting support operations for the war in Korea, so we had a lot of time at sea. Other than my two four-hour watches as officer of the deck, I had little to do, so I read and studied the Bible extensively. One day as I was studying, something in the text caused me to ask myself if I would be willing to serve with The Navigators at the end of my obligated service. I wrestled with this, not because of Christian service versus the business world, but because The Navigators is an interdenominational organization. The church I grew up in was very strong on "the local church only." I hesitated because of that, but I finally told the Lord I would be willing to serve with The Navigators if that is where He wanted me.

In October 1952, I had my annual physical and, as usual, passed. Then in December I became eligible for promotion to the next rank. Even though I had just had a physical in October, I had to take another one for my promotion. It was scheduled for December 26 at the naval hospital in Yokosuka.

Meanwhile, I had invited the two Navigator staff men to Christmas dinner at the officers' club on the base. During the meal, one of them asked me with a rather quaint expression, "Have you ever thought about throwing in your lot with us?" I responded that yes, I had thought about it, and he dropped the subject at that point because he had no authority to carry the conversation forward. I think he was seeking to plant a seed in my mind, only to discover that the seed had already been planted.

The next day I went to the naval hospital for my physical. Between October and that day, the hospital had received an audiometer, which gave more accurate hearing tests. I finally failed my hearing test, so my promotion was put on hold. Early in 1953 our ship returned to San Diego. While underway, I received orders to report to the naval hospital there for further testing. After a week of testing, the doctor determined that I had a 50 percent hearing loss, not enough in his opinion to disqualify me. However, the Bureau of Naval Personnel in Washington disagreed and asked me to resign my commission for medical reasons. I was finally discharged the first week in July 1953, after twenty-six months of active duty.

When I had signed up for the navy college program in 1947, the contract was for two years of active duty and six years of reserve duty. Because of the Korean War, the navy had unilaterally changed the contract to three years of active duty and five years of reserve, but I had served my original contract plus two months.

As I look back on twenty-six months of active duty, I ask, "What did God accomplish in my life during that time?"

The first thing was bringing me into contact with The Navigators very early in my active duty. This, of course, changed my future completely. The second thing I learned was to apply Scripture to specific situations in life. I mentioned we had six officers aboard the LST. The commanding officer was in his forties and had come up through the enlisted ranks during World War II. The remaining five of us ranged in age from twenty-two to twenty-five. In addition to the age gap, the commanding officer had almost no people skills, so we other officers had little respect for him and would often make fun of him behind his back.

One day, in my regular Bible study, I was studying 1 Timothy 6, and verse 1 says, "Let all who are under a yoke as bondservants regard their own masters as worthy of all honor, so that the name of God and the teaching may not be reviled."

When I read that verse I was immediately convicted of my dishonorable attitude toward the captain. I repented and changed my attitude so that I began to show him respect, deserved or not. Some months later, when I finally left the ship to be discharged, he took my hand and said, "Bridges, I really hate to see you go." There's another lesson to be learned from this one. Look for the principle behind the specific command. Obviously I was not a slave, or bondservant, to the commanding officer, but I was under his authority. And the principle behind Paul's specific command to slaves is to honor anyone in authority over us. This is how we learn to apply the Bible to our present-day lives.

The third lesson I learned was to study on my own because I did not have someone to disciple me. This was very valuable to me in later life as I began to write books on subjects usually beyond The Navigators' discipleship material.

The fourth lesson was learning to assume responsibility and to take the initiative in getting things done. That lesson proved invaluable to me during my years in administration at The Navigators headquarters.

CHAPTER 8

San Diego
Navigator Home

During the interval between our ship's arrival in San Diego and my discharge date, I had at last considerable contact with The Navigator representative responsible for The Navigators ministry in San Diego. He asked me to stay in San Diego and help in the ministry. In fact, he invited me to live in his home along with three other single men. This was the same home where I had first met The Navigators in December 1951. The house was not large, but it had a two-bedroom bunkhouse behind the main house. Each bedroom had a set of bunk beds so there was room for the four of us. We were on our own in the bunkhouse but had our evening meal and Sunday dinner with the family.

I had to get a job. San Diego had a lot of industry, particularly three aircraft firms. The largest was Convair, which employed about 17,000 people. With my good grades from engineering school, I assumed it would be easy enough to get a job at one of the three companies, but such was not the case. In addition to the three aircraft companies, I applied to other industries in the city but was getting no response. After about two weeks I became disgruntled with God for not providing a job for me — after all, I was in San Diego to serve Him. I knew the solution to my attitude was to be found in the Bible, but where? For some reason I decided to read Job. Actually, I skimmed through the various dialogues between Job and his three friends. Finally I came to chapter 34, and verses 18-19 nailed me:

> Is it fit to say to a king, Thou art wicked? and to princes, Ye are ungodly? How much less to him that accepteth not the persons of princes, nor regardeth the rich more than the poor? for they all are the work of his hands. (Job 34:18-19, KJV)

I was thunderstruck. It was as if God were saying to me, "Who do you think you are to accuse Me, the infinitely Holy God, of being unfair to you?" I was deeply convicted, fell on my knees, and repented to God. I don't want to suggest that the next event always happens in these situations, but within an hour I received a phone call from Convair asking me to come in for an interview, and I was hired immediately.

Let's consider this event as an illustration of God's providence. Could He have provided a job at Convair in two days instead of two weeks? Of course He could. But it seems that God wanted to teach me an invaluable lesson about complaining against Him, so He delayed the job interview for two weeks. It is often through a combination of Scripture and providential circumstances that God drives home to our hearts a lesson He wants us to learn deeply.

Complaining about God's seemingly unfair treatment is a common sin among Christians in the midst of difficult circumstances. As far back as the days of Job, the mysterious speaker Elihu said of Job, "For he has said, 'It profits a man nothing that he should take delight in God'" (34:9).

It is still true today, and I acknowledge there are times when I am tempted with this sin. But I am grateful that way back in 1953, God, through His providential workings, taught me a lesson about complaining against Him that still serves me today.

So I had my job but not a job I would have chosen. Instead, I was hired to develop and write test procedures for quality-control people to use in inspecting an airplane in its final assembly stage. When that project was completed, I was transferred to the service engineering department to write instructions for doing major repairs or modifications on aircraft already delivered to customers. Then finally, some of us were assigned to write a manual for teaching a description of all the operating systems of a new jet fighter plane yet to be delivered to the air force. I did not appreciate it at the time, but only years later when I began to write books did I realize God had been training me to write simply and concisely.

The primary ministry of the San Diego Navigators at that time was the Friday night meeting at the Navigator home. There were a number of shore bases in the San Diego area, plus all the ships present at any time in San Diego bay. Men came from many of these bases and ships, and the only way to have regular contact with them was through the Friday night meeting. After a large group gathering, we would divide up into different Bible studies.

I was asked to meet with the first-timers each week and give an overview of The Navigators' ministry and how it could benefit them. This was my first experience in public speaking, even to a small group, but it was God's first step in preparing me to speak to much larger groups later on (more on this in chapter 13).

My other main ministry experience was at a servicemen's center in downtown San Diego. It was a combination hospitality and evangelism center, and I was asked to go there each Saturday afternoon and evening to do follow-up with new converts. The center director, however, had other plans. He was not interested in follow-up. He just wanted us to do evangelism.

Most of the men who came into the center were eighteen- and nineteen-year-old recruits still undergoing basic training at both the Navy and Marine Corps Training Centers. They would fill up the center on Saturday afternoons in order to get the homemade refreshments supplied by women of local churches. About once an hour the director would get everyone's attention, and he or someone else would give a short evangelistic message of about ten minutes. Then the speaker would invite those who wanted to receive Christ to go into an adjoining room where someone would go over the assurance of salvation and pray with them.

I was asked to be one of those who regularly gave those

evangelistic messages, and I always had a dozen or more men who went into the prayer room at the end of the message. Looking back, however, I seriously question how many of those men were genuinely born again, rather than just responding to what I now consider to be high-pressure evangelism. But once again, God was using that experience to develop me in public preaching and teaching.

By the spring of 1955 I was restless. My Navigator representative was resigning to go into the pastorate, and without him I felt disconnected from The Navigators. I was eligible for thirty-six months of additional education through the GI Bill, which provided benefits for veterans of both World War II and the Korean War. I decided to explore going to seminary, so I sent to three schools asking for catalogues. As I looked through them, nothing excited me. That was God's way of closing that door. My theological education was to come later, but not from a seminary. Instead it was to come through studying the writings of older writers in the seventeenth, eighteenth, and nineteenth centuries.

CHAPTER 9

Glen Eyrie

In 1953 The Navigators purchased a property called Glen
Eyrie in Colorado Springs. In the summer of 1955, at the
time I was getting restless, they were recruiting men to
work on the project of expanding conference accommoda-
tions. I was aware of that but did not respond to it because
I had no skills for that kind of work. However, I did agree
to go to a conference at the Glen.

One night during the conference, God used something
the speaker said to convict me that I was backing off from
my commitment to serve with The Navigators if that is
what He wanted. After that evening meeting, I went out on
the lawn and spent time reflecting and praying to God
about my commitment. Finally, I renewed my commitment
to serve The Navigators in whatever capacity they wanted.

The next day I was asked to go to Dawson Trotman's
office. He was the founder and president of The Navigators,
but he was very much a "hands-on" person and made all the
personnel decisions. After we talked for a few minutes, he
told me of a need he had in the office, specifically someone to
supervise the correspondence department. At that time, that

department handled all incoming mail not addressed to a specific individual. As he described the job, my heart responded and I immediately told him that I would do it. I went back to San Diego, gave two weeks' notice, and returned to Colorado Springs about July 1, 1955. That was the beginning of my full-time service with The Navigators. So in high school, when the future was a blank, God took me by the hand and led me to college, to the navy, to contact with The Navigators, to His ultimate career destination for me, a lifetime of service with The Navigators.

But God's providential leading for me did not begin the evening in the spring semester of my senior year in high school. At some prior date He caused the US Navy to develop a new program for developing future navy officers through training them at civilian universities. The announcement of this plan was picked up and published by our local newspaper, and I happened to read the article.

God, who has purposed the end from the beginning, directs and orchestrates millions of events and circumstances every day. Obviously, I was not the only one to benefit from this new program. But it is fascinating and encouraging to realize that God is directing the events of our lives to accomplish His overall purposes. This is true of every believer. It is just as true of you as it is of me.

Several months before leaving San Diego, I had developed a mutual romantic relationship with a young woman involved in our ministry. I think we both assumed we would get married and go to a mission field with The Navigators. After I moved to Glen Eyrie, we continued to correspond by mail, but as the fall moved on, I became increasingly uncomfortable with continuing the relationship. The mental discomfort became so strong that I finally said to God one night, "I think You want me to break off this relationship, so tomorrow I will write a letter and do it." Immediately upon saying that, the mental discomfort disappeared.

This is one way the Holy Spirit guides us, causing a strong impression not to proceed in the direction we are going or, conversely, a strong impression that He wants us to do something. We will see an illustration of the latter toward the end of this chapter.

One of the first lessons I learned at Glen Eyrie concerned my giving commitment. As a single officer aboard ship, and later, still single working in industry with a good salary and few expenses, I developed a pattern of giving about half of my monthly income to The Navigators and my local church. However, in going to Glen Eyrie as a staff trainee, I took a tremendous drop in income. I was financially "shell-shocked." I barely had enough to cover necessary personal expenses.

I thought, "I can't afford to give. I will consider my 'sacrificial' service here at Glen Eyrie as my giving." God did not let me get away with that thinking. He wanted me to learn to give out of a meager income. We received eleven dollars a week in cash and were told that our food and lodging was valued at fifteen dollars, making a total of twenty-six dollars a week. So I decided to give three dollars a week, leaving me eight dollars for necessities — barely enough, and sometimes not enough, to get by on.

Another financial challenge was that, coming from San Diego, I had no winter coat. I had seen one in a store window for twenty-five dollars (remember, this is 1955), but I didn't have twenty-five dollars. However, a friend "out of the blue" sent me a check for twenty-five dollars. But in the same mail, I received a request for funds from a ministry I respected. As I prayed about it, I somehow sensed that God wanted me to send the entire twenty-five dollars to the ministry, which I did. A few weeks later I received another check for twenty-five dollars, this time from a missionary in Korea whom I had supported while in industry. With the check he enclosed a little note with Ecclesiastes 11:1 written on it: "Cast your bread upon the waters, for you will find it after many days." This time I was able to buy the coat. But through these events God was teaching me to give when I didn't think I could afford to give.

About this time I came across the story of the widow feeding Elijah, as recorded in 1 Kings 17:8-16. The widow was down to her last amount of flour and oil, and she was about to cook it for herself and her son and then die. And Elijah said to her, "Feed me first." But with that he gave her a promise that she would not run out of flour and oil. The story closes with the words of verse 16: "The jar of flour was not spent, neither did the jug of oil become empty, according to the word of the LORD that he spoke by Elijah." I began to pray over that verse, asking God to help me believe that through giving to Him first, my and my family's needs would always be met. That is what has happened for over fifty-five years.

In addition to our respective jobs at the Glen, we were in training. We had Bible studies, one-to-one times, and actual classes. The class I remember the most was the class on world missions. One of our assignments was to use our concordance and look up verses containing the words *nations, Gentiles,* and *the ends of the earth*. I found more than eighty, all the way from Genesis to Revelation. That is where I began to have a heart for world missions.

Since I had terminated my relationship with the young lady in San Diego, I assumed God would bring another one in her place. But months went by and it didn't happen. In early 1957 I was spending some time in Psalm 116. I was especially drawn to verse 7: "Return, O my soul, to your rest; for the LORD has dealt bountifully with you." As I prayed over it I had a sense that God was saying to me something such as, "I have marriage plans for you, and when it happens you will say, 'The Lord has indeed dealt bountifully with me.'" The impression was so strong that I wrote that day's date in the margin of my Bible, something I seldom do.

But as the months wore on and nothing happened, I began to question if God had really spoken to me that day through that verse. By the time I left for Europe (see next chapter), I had completely dismissed it from my mind. This, as you might guess, was not the end of the story, but for that you will have to wait until the end of the next chapter.

Going back to the night when I asked God to use the Bible to guide my conduct, at that time I assumed I would just read in the Bible what I was supposed to do and do it.

Simple as that. I was naively unaware of the conflict
between the flesh and the Spirit (see Galatians 5:17), so I
found myself failing often, but I plowed on thinking it was
all up to me and my willpower.

Now back to Glen Eyrie, about 1957. Somehow a teaching infiltrated the staff at Glen Eyrie which taught that just
as we do nothing for our salvation, so we do nothing for our
sanctification. Instead, we just ask Jesus to live His life
through us. We are completely passive.

Coming from a do-it-yourself approach to obedience,
this was like a new chapter of the gospel to me. I bought
into it completely. Another aspect of the teaching, based on
Romans 6:11, is that if you reckon yourself dead to sin, you
will no longer sin. This teaching completely misunderstood
the truth that we are dead to the dominion of sin but not to
the activity of sin in our lives. Nevertheless, I was trying to
reckon myself dead to sin and still seeing sin in my life.

One night I was looking at Romans 6:11, maybe in light
of some sinful failures that day. As I looked at the verse, the
thought came into my mind, "It isn't true, is it?" I said to
myself, "No, it isn't." The next thought that came was,
"How do you know that John 3:16 is true?" Fortunately I
recognized this as a direct satanic attack on the truthfulness
of Scripture. I immediately fell on my knees and prayed,
"God, whatever happens, don't let me lose my faith."

Shortly after that, through additional Bible study in
Romans 6–8, I came to realize the passive approach was not
biblical. Through these twists and turns in my own life, I
finally came to a principle which I articulate as the principle

of *dependent responsibility*. We are responsible. We cannot just let Jesus live His life through us, but at the same time we are dependent. We cannot make one inch of progress in the Christian life apart from the enabling power of the Holy Spirit. This became a major emphasis in my teaching.

One evening I was reading in the Minor Prophets and was struck by God's judgment on the disobedient nation of Israel. Then I began to reflect on God's love for me in the truth that Christ had suffered on the cross to deliver me from God's judgment. As I thought on this I "heard" the inaudible voice of God as He planted these thoughts in my mind:

> "Jerry, do you believe I love you?"
> "Yes, Lord, I've just been reflecting on Your love for me."
> "Do you believe that I love you just as you are?"
> "Yes, Lord. I am so grateful that You love me just as I am."
> "Do you believe that I love Jim Smith?" (not his real name)

Now, Jim Smith was a fellow staff member that I had trouble liking, let alone loving. So I had to think about that for a moment before I finally said,

> "Yes, Lord. I believe that You love Jim Smith."
> "Do you believe that I love Jim Smith just as he is?"

I was, as it were, painted into a corner, so I replied,

"Yes, Lord. I believe that You love Jim Smith just as
    he is."

Now the Lord drove home His lesson for me.

"If I love Jim Smith just as he is, can you?"

At the time of this experience I was still under the
influence of the "Just let Jesus live His life through you"
approach to Christian living, so I said,

"Lord, I cannot, but I'm willing to let Jesus love
    him through me."

That was not a good answer. I should have said something like, "Lord, I'm willing to, but I cannot just decide to
love Jim. Will You, through Your Spirit, enable me to love
him as You do?"

It may not surprise you to learn that, over time, Jim and
I became good friends. Though my prayer was based on what
I now consider to be bad theology, God answered the intent
of the prayer and so worked in my heart that Jim and I developed a mutual friendship. In fact, we later worked together
on some key office projects.

God taught me a valuable lesson that night that has
served me well ever since. Sometimes I receive a stinging
and hurtful letter from someone who strongly disagrees

with the overall message of one of my books. Now I pray something such as, "Lord, he is Your child and my brother in Christ. You love him just as You love me. Would You bless him? And may we both come to a greater understanding of Your Word."

I believe this truth, that we are fellow members of the body of Christ and that God loves each of us, could serve to diffuse a lot of hostility and disagreement among fellow believers. I am grateful that God taught me this lesson early in my training to be a Navigator staff member.

Could God have taught me this lesson directly from the Scriptures, apart from the experience of hearing His "inaudible" voice? Certainly He could. This truth, in one way or another, is taught throughout the Bible. So why the "inaudible" voice experience? I don't know. Perhaps it was because I was too dense to learn it any other way. In any event, any such experience that we have must ultimately be supported by Scripture and be only an application of Scripture to one's life or an increased understanding of Scripture.

Another truth I had somehow missed was that of our living union with Christ as depicted by Jesus in His illustration of the vine and the branches in John 15. In the summer of 1956, for some reason, I was discouraged. Walking along a path at Glen Eyrie, I said to myself, "How can someone in Christ be as miserable as I am?" Immediately the thought came into my mind, "What did you just say? What does it mean to be in Christ?" To me, the term "in Christ" meant no more than being a Christian, but that morning I went to one of my favorite outdoor places for time alone with God and began to ponder that question. Numerous verses with those short words "in Christ" began to scroll through my mind. Gradually, it dawned on me that to be "in Christ" meant to be so spiritually united to Him that His life and power could naturally flow into and through me. That was my first exposure to the whole concept of *union with Christ*. There is a second aspect of our union with Christ that we will look at in a later chapter.

Dawson Trotman died in a boat accident on June 19, 1956, and Lorne Sanny became president of The Navigators. Contrary to Dawson's hands-on method of operation, Lorne was a delegator, so he began to assemble a team to work at The Navigators headquarters. Meanwhile, a veteran Navigator from the 1930s navy days, Jim Downing, had retired and he came to assist Sanny in the operation of Glen Eyrie and the headquarters. Because of my service as an officer in the Korean War, he selected me to be his assistant, and I was asked to become part of the permanent headquarters staff.

In retrospect this was a blessing. Though most everyone can disciple others on a one-to-one basis, not everyone is gifted to lead a Navigator ministry. Therefore, a number of people who were invited to Glen Eyrie for training never became Navigator staff. I probably would have been one of those people. So, God kept me in The Navigators through putting me into an administrative role.

Another event illustrated the importance of God putting us in roles we are suited for and keeping us from roles where we would fail. In the summer of 1959, one of the leaders approached me about the possibility of going to Germany to take charge of one of the servicemen's centers. A Navigators servicemen's center was actually a combination of a hospitality center and a discipleship center. It involved gifting both in hospitality, meaning in this case, food, and the ability to disciple men in the process. Fortunately for me, The Navigators decided to send someone else. I would have been a miserable failure, particularly in the hospitality part.

At the beginning of 1959, I was asked to become manager of the buildings and grounds at Glen Eyrie. I could manage well enough, but, to use an analogy from my navy days, I had no chief petty officer to handle the technical details. Consequently, it turned out to be a very challenging year for me.

In September 1959, two of us at Glen Eyrie were given a free scholarship to the Dale Carnegie Public Speaking Course. The course was one night a week from seven to eleven p.m. for fourteen weeks. Every week we had to give two two-minute speeches, each of them designed to teach a specific lesson in public speaking. The course was invaluable, and I would say that whatever ability I have in preaching and teaching today can be traced back to that course. But why was I chosen to be the recipient of one of those two scholarships? It was because the One who took me by the hand as a seventeen-year-old was still holding my hand and bringing me along the path He had marked out for me.

In November 1959, one Sunday evening, I had a strong mental impression that I should write my dad a letter, thanking him for all that he had meant to me in my growing-up years. I thought to myself, "Yes, that's a good idea. I'll do it tomorrow." I went to bed, but I could not go to sleep. The impression that I should write my dad grew so strong that I finally got up out of bed, wrote the letter, addressed and sealed the envelope, and went back to bed. I mailed the letter the next morning. Dad probably received the letter on Wednesday or Thursday. The following Sunday he had a massive heart attack, and though he did not die immediately, he was not able to communicate when I finally got to Tyler to see him. Dad lived a few more weeks and finally died on December 21. Actually, I was preparing to drive to Tyler with a friend the next day when I received the call from Dad's boss that he had died. I had just turned thirty on December 4. So with my mother's death when I was fourteen, I was essentially "orphaned" by the time I was thirty. But as I would learn later, this too was part of God's plan for me.

Now I could easily see why I had the strong impression to write the letter of thanks. I know that some people do not put much value in impressions, as they are too subjective. But I have to say that the two instances recounted in this chapter, first to write the letter to terminate the romantic relationship, and second, to write the letter to my dad, obviously had to be the work of the Holy Spirit.

The Scripture is quite clear that we are to honor our father and mother (see Ephesians 6:2), and Jesus makes it clear in Mark 7:9-13 that this commandment applies to adults as well as children. I realized later in life that I had failed in this commandment; not that I had dishonored my father, but that I had failed to honor him through frequent communications. So I am grateful that the Holy Spirit would not let me rest that night in November 1959 until I had written that letter of appreciation to my dad.

In early December, before Dad's death, I asked for an appointment with Lorne Sanny. I went in and said, "Sanny, I have two things to say. First, I am willing to stay in this job as long as you want me to. Second, I am unhappy in it." He said, "I'm glad you came in. I have another job for you."

He had just returned from Europe and had learned that his newly appointed Europe director was bogged down with administration. He came home determined to find someone to go and meet that need. This is what he proposed to me that morning. I had mixed feelings. For one thing, I had just turned thirty and was still single with no prospects. He told me that he was thinking of another staff member in addition to me, so I hoped the other staff member would get the assignment.

As I prayed about my own response, I had the increasing conviction that God wanted me to go. The Scripture God used was Hebrews 11:8: "By faith Abraham, when he was called to go out into a place which he should after receive for an inheritance, obeyed; and he went out, not knowing whither he went" (KJV). The words that stood out to me were "by faith Abraham . . . obeyed." I finally said, "Lord, if You want me to go as a single man, by faith I will obey You and trust You for whatever You have for me in the future." I was asked to take the assignment and so made preparation to go.

CHAPTER 10

Europe

The Navigators Missions Director was a very frugal man, and he set my monthly budget at $150 plus $300 cash needed for my transportation to Europe. Keep in mind that this was 1960. I, of course, had to raise this money. I went to Texas to visit my stepmother and it *just so happened* that there was a one-day Navigator men's conference in the area. I went to the conference, and they made my cash need their offering project. At the end of the day, the emcee announced that the total received in the offering was $299.75. Someone stood up and tossed a quarter to the emcee, so my cash need was met to the penny.

From Texas I went to San Diego to raise monthly support. On Sunday I went to the church where I had been a member. As I walked out, a friend, an older lady, handed me a booklet and said, "I want you to read this." I took it and put it in my jacket pocket. That afternoon I remembered it and retrieved it from the jacket. The title of the booklet was *The Doctrine of Election.* I had never heard of the doctrine before, but it was so contrary to my beliefs that I was deeply offended. I said to myself, "She has gotten into heresy." I set the booklet aside and had no intention of pursuing the subject any further.

The next morning I was having an extended time with God. In the course of that time, a series of thoughts came to my mind so clearly that I still remember them over fifty years later. Here they are:

"How many people are in San Diego?"
My answer: "About 600,000" (in 1960).
"How many of them do you think are believers?"
My answer: "No more than 10 percent, say
    60,000."
"You are one of them, aren't you?"
"Yes, Lord, and I'm so grateful that I am."
"Why?" (That is, why are you one of them?)

Immediately the booklet that I had read made sense and I saw that I was a believer because God had chosen me (see Ephesians 1:4).

My immediate reaction was to fall on my knees as Romans 12:1 came to mind. "I appeal to you therefore, brothers, by the mercies of God, to present your bodies as a living sacrifice, holy and acceptable to God, which is your spiritual worship." I prayed, "Lord, I have offered myself to You before, but in light of a deeper understanding of Your mercy and grace, I present myself once more." You might say that in "the twinkling of an eye" I was changed from a non-Calvinist to what I learned later was a Calvinist. (Calvinism is named after John Calvin, one of the sixteenth-century reformers. It is also known as Reformed Theology.)

What is a Calvinist? The answer to that is well beyond the scope of this book, but to me the most basic answer is that a Calvinist believes in the sovereignty of God in all things, including the salvation of sinners. Jesus said in John 3:3-8 that to see the kingdom of God, one must be born again. How and when does this happen?

Calvinists believe that all people are born spiritually dead (see Ephesians 2:1) and do not have the ability to believe in Christ apart from the regenerating work of the Holy Spirit. For all those whom God has chosen, or "elected," the Holy Spirit comes and sovereignly gives spiritual life. The person is born again and, as a result, his spiritual eyes are open and he believes the gospel and trusts in Christ as Savior.

The Calvinist also believes in the genuine free offer of the gospel to everyone. He takes seriously Scriptures such as Romans 10:13, for "everyone who calls on the name of the Lord will be saved." He does not try to reconcile the free offer with the doctrine of election. He believes the Bible teaches both and leaves the reconciliation to God.

By contrast, the non-Calvinist believes that by grace God gives all people the ability to believe or not to believe the gospel, and it is a person's free choice to believe or not believe. Once a person believes, he or she is born again.

I realize this is a controversial subject, and in the body of Christ as a whole probably the majority of believers would consider themselves non-Calvinists if they knew the issues. This includes many of my dear friends and

colaborers in The Navigators. I have never tried to per-
suade a non-Calvinist to become a Calvinist, and I'm not
trying to do so in mentioning this event, but I cannot tell
my story of God's leading in my life without including it,
because it was a watershed event for me. It eventually
changed my whole outlook about God, the world, and the
gospel. In fact, this one event eventually led to my clear
understanding of the sovereignty of God and the providence of God, which is the primary subject of this book.

A few weeks later I left for Europe aboard a transatlan-
tic ship. The journey from New York to France was about a
week. During that time I read through most of the New
Testament and, with my new perspective, saw the doctrine
of election all throughout the Scriptures. This is an important point because our experiences, as real as they may be,
must always be validated by the Scriptures. Today, if someone were to ask me why I believe in God's sovereign election, I would not say, because I had an experience in 1960,
but because I believe that is what the Bible teaches.

My friend back in San Diego was an avid reader of the
Puritans. When she learned what had happened to me, she
began to send me Puritan books. Over the next three years,
I studied the Bible and the Puritans. As a result, I became a
committed Calvinist, but I hope a friendly Calvinist toward
those who have a different view.

One of the books my friend sent me was a large Puritan
tome titled *The Existence and Attributes of God*, by the Puritan
pastor Stephen Charnock. Because of my strong interest in
the subject of personal holiness, I turned immediately to

the chapter called "The Holiness of God." I began reading, and after just a few pages I found myself spontaneously on my knees before this infinitely holy God. I got up and began to read again, but after a few pages I again found myself on my knees before God.

This experience, one of God's unusual providences in my life, had a profound and lasting influence on my view of God, but also on my view of myself. Through it I began to see something of the depth of my own sinful depravity. I could relate to Isaiah, who when he saw God in His infinite holiness, immediately cried out, "Woe is me! For I am lost; for I am a man of unclean lips . . . for my eyes have seen the King, the LORD of hosts!" (Isaiah 6:5).

I believe this event set me up for my realization, some years later, of the necessity of Christians to live by the gospel every day of our lives, even if we are not aware of any so-called "major sins" in our lives. Like Isaiah, we need to continually hear the words of the gospel, "Your guilt is taken away, and your sin atoned for" (6:7).

Now let's move on to my time in Europe. Though I landed in France, my ultimate destination was Holland, where the Europe director lived. The Dutch Navigators had scheduled a one-day conference on the Saturday after I arrived and had asked the Europe director to give the main messages through a translator. About Thursday night he informed me that he had a terrible sore throat and would not be able to speak. I would have to take his place. Welcome to Holland!

There were probably a hundred or so people at the

conference. I had never spoken to a group that large before, but this was of God, who was developing in me over time the gift of public teaching and preaching. In recent years I have given over one hundred messages each year.

Again we see the providential hand of God at work. Our director was such a compelling speaker that I am not sure, if he had not been laid aside, there would have ever been an opportunity for me to get experience in speaking, at least in Europe. As it turned out, toward the end of my three-year assignment, he and I would sometimes share the speaking at a weekend conference.

At that time the Europe director was responsible for the ministries among nationals in about seven countries and also the U.S. military in Germany and Italy. He asked me to be responsible for the military ministry in Germany. Again, I was in over my head. My military ministry experience in San Diego consisted of evangelism and basic discipleship. I had no experience in leading a ministry, so I really had nothing to offer the local military staff in Germany. Fortunately, this predicament did not last long. The Navigators leadership in the States decided to separate the military from the national ministries (a good decision, by the way). They sent a man experienced in military ministry in the States to direct that ministry in Europe. Here again, I can see the providential hand of God delivering me from a responsibility in which I would have likely failed. In God's leading in our lives, it is just as important that He keep us from the wrong ministry as that He directs us to the right one.

Back in Holland I had a small man-to-man ministry

with a few university students who spoke excellent English, but midway through my three-year term, the director of the Dutch ministry wanted to conduct it all in the Dutch language. I heartily agreed with this decision, but it left me without any personal ministry.

But again God worked. There was an American Air Force squadron on a Dutch airbase about an hour's drive from where we lived. The chaplain of the squadron invited me to lead a Bible study for both couples and single men each Monday night, so on Monday afternoons I drove to the base, met one-on-one with one of the airmen who was a new Christian, and then led the Bible study. About nine p.m. I would start the hour's drive back home. It was during that time that Satan began to unleash his attacks on me.

As a whole, things were not going well with me. As a single man, I was lonely. I was struggling with some issues in my personal life, and there was occasionally tension between the director and me. Using these issues, Satan began to attack me. "Who do you think you are, seeking to minister to these people when you have so many issues yourself? Why, you probably aren't even a Christian."

In desperate self-defense I began to resort to the gospel. Isaiah 53:6, "All we like sheep have gone astray; we have turned — every one — to his own way; and the LORD has laid on him the iniquity of us all," became a lifeline for me. I began to sing some of the old gospel hymns I remembered from childhood. Hymns such as "Just As I Am" and "Rock of Ages" would go through my mind, and through resorting to the gospel, I defended myself against Satan.

Unfortunately, during that time I didn't see the principle behind all this, that not only I but all Christians should be living by the gospel every day. It would be fifteen years before I began to teach this important truth to others.

At some point in my three-year term I was confronted with the doctrine of sinless perfection, a state that a believer enters through a second blessing of the Holy Spirit. The article promoting this teaching was very persuasive, particularly citing the experience of godly men of the past, all whose names would have been well known among evangelical Christians at that time. I thought, "Can all these godly men be wrong?" but I prayed, "Lord, show me from the Scriptures whether this is true or not." Almost immediately there came into my mind the episode where Paul rebuked Peter because of his cowardice and hypocrisy (see Galatians 2:11-14).

I thought to myself, "If ever there was someone baptized by the Holy Spirit, it was Peter on the day of Pentecost (see Acts 2), yet in Galatians 2, he is sinning." Immediately the issue was settled for me. The Word of God trumps the experience of people, regardless of how godly they may be. Here is the principle to draw from this episode: We must always be like the Bereans, who gladly listened to Paul, then examined the Scriptures daily to see if what he said was true (see Acts 17:11).

Answers from Scripture do not always come so easily and quickly as they did for me in Holland. By contrast, back at Glen Eyrie in the late 1950s, I wrestled for months with the "just let Jesus live His life through you" teaching.

I was scheduled to return to the States in March 1963.

I wanted to spend two days sightseeing, so I wrote to Eleanor Miller, a Navigator associate staff in New York, asking her to try to find a reasonably priced hotel in Manhattan for me and, of course, giving her my arrival date. At the close of the letter, I added a P.S.: "How about having dinner with me for old time's sake, on the day I arrive."

I had met Eleanor the summer of 1955 at Glen Eyrie, though I was not particularly impressed. For one thing, I was still interested in the young woman in San Diego, but in addition, Eleanor was a soprano soloist who often sang at Glen Eyrie conference meetings. She was a gifted singer, but her classical style put me off, because I was still outgrowing my background of country gospel music from my teenage years in east Texas. Over the next four years we had varying degrees of contact at Glen Eyrie but never really got to know each other, though I did learn to appreciate her singing. In the fall of 1959, she moved to New York City to be part of a team of Navigator women ministering to single women in the city. In January of 1960 I went to Europe, and we had no contact for over three years.

One night after mailing the letter to Eleanor asking for her help with the hotel room and inviting her to have dinner with me, I was praying about my return to the States and to The Navigators office at Glen Eyrie. I knew then I would be working around single women as I had in the 1950s, and during that time no romance had ever developed, despite my desires for such. So that night I prayed something like this: "God, I am willing to be single the rest of my life, but if that is Your plan for me, would You somehow let me know it so that I can just close the door of my heart on that subject?" Immediately words came to my mind: "What about that promise I gave you?" I then remembered the day in 1957 when God had impressed so strongly on my mind Psalm 116:7: "Return, O my soul, to your rest; for the LORD has dealt bountifully with you." I had written the date in the margin of my Bible.

I knew that had been in the early spring, about the same time I would be returning to the States, so I said to the Lord, "Wouldn't it be great if You would begin to fulfill that promise on the anniversary of the date You gave it to me?" The next question, of course, was what was that exact date? I was no longer using the Bible I had used in 1957, so I had to dig it out of my footlocker. As I turned to Psalm 116, I was astonished to see that it was March 17, the date I would be arriving in New York and meeting Eleanor for dinner. I was stunned, so I said, "Lord, is this a coincidence or are You trying to tell me something?" Immediately Psalm 118:24 came to my mind: "This is the day that the LORD has made; let us rejoice and be glad in it."

I said, "Lord, I have no interest in Eleanor. If this is from You, You will have to give me one." Over the intervening weeks, between that night and March 17, an interest began to grow in my heart.

I don't often share this story, for two reasons. First, I don't want people to get the impression that the Christian life should be a series of dramatic encounters with God. It certainly has not been with me. The two instances in this chapter, the one concerning election at the beginning of the chapter and the one about Eleanor, are unusual and not representative of the way God usually works in our lives. More often, He works through a series of commonplace events. The second reason I do not often share this story is because it is extraordinary and does not represent the way God usually brings a man and woman together. I used to wonder, "Lord, why did this happen this way?" I concluded that the Lord was probably showing me that He is not limited to ordinary ways and, further, that He was through grace rewarding my faith of three years before when, based on Abraham's example in Hebrews 11:8, I went to Europe having no idea if and how God would ever work out marriage for me.

CHAPTER 11

Early Married Life

I did have dinner with Eleanor on March 17, 1963, the day I arrived back in the States and also the anniversary of the date when I felt God had given me a promise six years before from Psalm 116:7. She gave me a brief tour of downtown Manhattan, and then we went to a restaurant in the Empire State Building for dinner. During dinner I asked her if she was romantically interested in anyone, and she said no. I then asked if she would be interested in our writing to one another to see if God might be bringing us together. She said yes. I did not know until after we were engaged that God had already prepared her heart in an unusual way. (I realize developing a relationship through letters sounds quaint today, but this was 1963. There were no computers or cell phones, and long-distance calls were still expensive.)

Since I was staying over the next day to do some more sightseeing, we arranged to have dinner the next evening. I then left for Houston, Texas, to visit my brother and family, then on to Tyler to visit my stepmother before heading back to Colorado Springs and The Navigators office. While in Houston, I spoke Sunday evening at my brother's church.

I spoke from Ecclesiastes 7:13, "Consider the work of God: who can make straight what he has made crooked?" and I talked about the sovereignty of God and accepting His work in our lives, whether good or bad. After the service, while getting into my brother's car, I tore a new jacket I had just received. God was giving me an opportunity to practice what I had just preached.

When I arrived at The Navigators office, I was asked to become the administrator of the missions department. Our missions director at the time was a pastor at heart and did a great job of pastoring our missionaries. However, he had no skills or interest in administration, so I filled a vital need.

Of course, my main interest in those days was developing a relationship with Eleanor. We concluded that the time in New York had been too short and that we should get together again. We agreed to meet at her parents' home in Pittsburgh over Memorial Day weekend. The problem for me, however, was that I had no money for the airfare. One day, out of the blue, I received a letter from my brother's church containing an honorarium for the service I had spoken at several weeks before. I was surprised because I had never before received an honorarium and didn't realize that guest speakers usually receive one. The important thing, though, was the amount of the check. It was almost exactly the cost of a roundtrip airfare to Pittsburgh. This was a further confirmation that God was at work bringing us together.

Eleanor's dad loaned me his car while we were there, so we had lots of time to be alone and talk. Both of us were scheduled to return to our respective jobs on Monday, so on

Sunday night I proposed to her. She did not say yes but said she would pray about it. She wasn't just putting me off. She really needed more confirmation from God that He was in this relationship. Finally, on June 19, about three weeks later, she called and accepted my proposal. We set the wedding date for October 19 at her home church in Pittsburgh.

Meanwhile, I had bought a 1958 Ford sedan. After only two weeks I had to have some major repairs on the engine. The mechanic told me that I should never again drive it over 55 mph. As the wedding date approached, I realized I had to drive this car about 5,000 miles going to Pittsburgh and returning via Mississippi and Texas, all at only a maximum speed of 55 mph. I had rented an apartment to bring Eleanor back to. The morning I was leaving for Pittsburgh, as I closed the front door of the apartment, Genesis 28:15 came to mind: "Behold, I am with you and will keep you wherever you go, and will bring you back to this land. For I will not leave you until I have done what I have promised you." It was as if God was encouraging me about the 5,000-mile trip, letting me know that He would take care of us. That is exactly what happened. In all that travel, I spent thirty-five dollars on two minor repairs.

There are two lessons to learn from God's bringing Genesis 28:15 to my mind that day. First, it demonstrates the importance of memorizing key Scriptures so that they are stored away in our minds, available for the Holy Spirit to bring them to our conscious minds as needed. Second, it shows the importance of memorizing and living by God's promises as well as His commands. The psalmist said, "I have stored up your word in my heart, that I might not sin against you" (Psalm 119:11). This principle of storing up God's Word in our hearts for future use applies not only to God's precepts but also to His promises.

We arrived back in Colorado Springs in mid-November of 1963, and I settled back into my job in the missions department. In the summer of 1964, however, The Navigators leadership made a major change. For one thing, they realized that the Glen Eyrie Training Program was not as effective as Dawson Trotman envisioned it to be. They realized the best training had to be done out in the ministry areas. In addition, the financial condition of the combined headquarters and Glen Eyrie was deteriorating. Some people had to be let go. I volunteered to leave my job, because I felt a capable secretary could do my work. At the same time, our midwest regional director was looking for somebody to begin a new ministry in the Kansas City community. Eleanor and I agreed to accept that role. So in September 1964, after being married only ten months, we packed up our possessions in a U-Haul trailer and headed for Kansas City. Somewhere out on the plains of eastern Colorado or western Kansas, we stopped for gas. For some reason, I walked around the car. As I did so, I noticed a big bubble on the right rear tire. Because we were in the gas station (which in those days was full-service), we managed to replace the tire without even unhooking the trailer or digging into the car trunk for the spare. Again, it seemed that God, through His providence, was looking out for us.

The U.S. Ministries director had told me, "Go to Kansas

City, get a job, begin to build a ministry, and work yourself into a full-time ministry role." The businessman who had asked The Navigators to send someone to Kansas City hired me. I learned later that he had an agenda that was more than providing a job for The Navigators staff man new in town. He wanted to get rid of his office manager, and he viewed me as the replacement. So after six weeks of trying to learn the business, I was suddenly in charge of both the office and the warehouse operations. Again, I was in over my head. I was working long hours just to keep up and had no time or energy to pioneer a ministry, so I became quite discouraged. In fact, one day I said to Eleanor, "We will be out of The Navigators within six months."

Shortly after that, I arrived home from work and Eleanor handed me a letter and said, "You need to sit down to read this." It was a letter from Lorne Sanny saying that the present office manager at headquarters had decided that he and his family wanted to go to the mission field, and they needed someone to replace him. Lorne asked us to pray about my being that person. He said if we returned, we should be there by July.

So we had to make a major decision, and I learned from that experience that all of our nice formulas for finding the will of God didn't work. Our regional director and my peers in the midwest region and the pastor of the church we were attending were all unanimous that we should stay in Kansas City, but we could not get settled about that option.

One day as I was driving in our car I prayed, "God, I don't know if You want us to remain in Kansas City or return to The Navigators headquarters, but one thing I know: I want to have a part in the Great Commission." Immediately the thought came to my mind, "How do you think you can have the greatest part?"

In wrestling with the question of how I could make the greatest impact, I reviewed all the assignments that I had had since college days. I realized that in every instance I had some administrative responsibility. I concluded that administration is where I could make the greatest contribution, so I said to the Lord, "I will go home and share this with Eleanor, and if she agrees, we will decide to return to Colorado Springs." So in early July 1965, just ten months after leaving Glen Eyrie, we returned, again with a U-Haul trailer. I did not know at the time that Eleanor was pregnant and had a difficult time during the trip. Our first child, Kathy, was born February 7, 1966. By this time Eleanor and I were both thirty-six years old.

I wondered why God would send us to Kansas City for such a short time. I finally realized that my job as the office manager of that business was really a cram course to prepare me for managing the headquarters office. In removing us from Kansas City, God, once again, kept me from failure in The Navigators ministry. I mentioned this to a friend, who responded, "But doesn't the providence of God include times of failure?" My answer was, "Yes." But if I had failed in Kansas City, we would have left The Navigators, and for reasons unknown to me at the time, God was keeping us in The Navigators.

We moved into a duplex apartment, where we were

living when Kathy was born. It was much too small and we had an opportunity to rent a full-size, three-bedroom house only a couple of miles from Glen Eyrie, so we moved again. In less than three years of married life, we had lived in three apartments and now a house. We thought we would stay there awhile, but after less than a year the owners notified us they were returning to Colorado Springs and would want their house.

I was tired of continually moving, so we decided to take advantage of veteran's benefits, which guaranteed veterans' loans with no down payment required. Using this benefit, we were able to buy a brand-new three-bedroom house with about a thousand square feet only three miles from Glen Eyrie. We moved into the house in the early summer of 1967, and our second child, Dan, was born September 25. Meanwhile, life at the office was pretty ordinary, and I felt comfortable in my new role. During that time I initiated three significant changes.

The first was to centralize our receipting process at headquarters. Up to that time all receipting for gifts to staff in the United States had been handled locally by the staff. This was not only cumbersome but also prevented our having a centralized record of each donor's gifts in case they were audited by the IRS.

The second was to go to a computer for all our data processing. I know this seems very ordinary today, but in 1967 it was a big step for us, involving a major expense and lots of training.

The third significant change affected the housing of

single staff. During the Glen Eyrie Training Program era, 1955–1964, all single staff lived on Glen Eyrie because they were involved in the training program. With the end of that program in the summer of 1964, there was no longer a reason for single staff to continue living on Glen Eyrie, so we encouraged them to move into town and get involved in local ministries. At first this was detrimental to the Glen Eyrie Conference Center because they lost the food and lodging income from these people. But in the long run it was a positive move because it freed up housing space for more conferees.

I know these changes seem very reasonable today, but believe me, the first and third of these changes were not without criticism at that time, though today they would be universally accepted. But I learned early on that most major changes result in criticism from some quarters.

When Eleanor and I returned in the summer of 1965, we joined the Evangelical Presbyterian Church, which had a fairly close relationship with The Navigators. Shortly after we became members, I was asked to teach an adult Sunday school class, and I continued to do that for ten years. Through this God was continuing to develop my teaching skills. I finally stopped teaching in 1976 because I was starting to write, but that is a subject for the next chapter.

In those days, leaders in the office often wore two or more hats. Jim Downing had a number of responsibilities, one being the corporate secretary and treasurer. He needed to be relieved of the day-to-day responsibility of that job but still have overall authority over the finances, so he became the financial vice president, and I became the corporate secretary and treasurer. That was in 1969 and was the beginning of a ten-year period that I regard as the most fulfilling period in almost forty years of administration with The Navigators.

CHAPTER 12

Secretary/Treasurer

As the secretary and treasurer I had two major responsibilities: legal and finance. As treasurer I had, among
other duties, the responsibility for properly insuring our
assets, of which Glen Eyrie was a major portion. I had to
make sure that both our property and liability coverages
were adequate. Today this is called risk management and is
a separate department at The Navigators office, but during
my time it was handled by me and an executive assistant.

Another area that fell to me was staff (employee) benefits, such as group health insurance, life insurance, and a
retirement plan. Normally these functions would be under a
human resources department, but since we had none at that
time, I inherited that responsibility. So, in summary, I was
responsible for four major areas:

- Legal affairs, including compliance with all state and
  federal laws and regulations
- The day-to-day operations of our finance
  department, including both the receipting and
  handling of donor income, and the accounting

department, including the annual audit
- Property and liability insurance
- Staff benefits

During my time as secretary/treasurer we were able to make some significant improvements in each of these areas.

But before I get into these improvements, I want to put this in the context of two Scripture verses. The first is 1 Peter 4:11: "Whoever serves, as one who serves by the strength that God supplies." The second verse is Isaiah 26:12, which in the NIV says, "LORD, you establish peace for us; all that we have accomplished you have done for us." Taken together, these verses teach us that whatever our role is, we are dependent on God's enabling power, and at the end of the day we can only say, "God has done this." So when I list some of our accomplishments during that ten-year period, my intent is to give glory to God and not to any individual, especially myself.

The legal affairs were fairly routine and consisted mostly of various legal contracts. The greater issue was compliance with all state and federal laws and regulations. I'm not sure about this, but it seems as if the Nav leadership had operated under the assumption that, as a nonprofit organization, The Navigators were not subject to such laws as the Fair Labor Standards Act (forty-hour work weeks and overtime pay for any hours in excess of forty). I myself was totally unaware of what our corporate obligations were.

One day, quite unintentionally, I learned that we were not in compliance with a law in every state that requires organizations operating in but not headquartered in that state to be registered as out-of-state corporations. Upon learning this through an incident with one state, we learned this is the law for all of the states. Immediately we set to work to register in every state where we had a Navigator ministry, which was at that time about three-fourths of the states. After this, I thought I had better inquire if there were other laws and regulations in which we were out of compliance. I contacted the attorney I was working with at that time. He went through the various laws and regulations and gave me a list of the ones we needed to be in compliance with.

The toughest one for the staff was the Fair Labor Standards Act. This was especially hard on the Glen Eyrie Conference Center, because most of their staff were working far more than forty hours a week and not getting paid for it. Coming into compliance obviously cost Glen Eyrie a significant amount of money.

The second law was unemployment compensation. The typical company has to pay into a state unemployment compensation fund, regardless of their track record of unemployment. In most states, however, we were able to opt for a "pay as you go" system. In other words, we paid into the state fund only when we had an employee claim in that particular state. A few states, however, did not offer a "pay as you go" plan, so we had to pay into the state unemployment compensation fund. Since The Navigators did not have at that time an administrative overhead fund, those charges had to be made to the staff accounts in those states. You may have heard an old saying that goes something like, "Shoot the messenger who brings bad news." Because of this human tendency, I was blamed for these extra charges when the fact was I was only getting us to comply with the laws that we should have been complying with for years.

The area in which I felt most fulfilled was that of staff benefits. Among other things, we were able to change our health-insurance plan to a self-insured fund, which significantly reduced our cost.

One day, as treasurer, I was looking over the budget and saw an expense for a retirement fund. I was not aware of what that was. Upon investigation I found it was indeed a small retirement fund so grossly inadequate that I would be embarrassed to put it in print. I went to my boss, Jim Downing, and then to the finance committee of the board and said in effect, "We need an adequate retirement plan." After my presentation, the finance committee said, "We agree with you. Go start one." Of course, I had no background or knowledge in this area, so I contacted a friend who was the human resources director for a fairly large corporation in the city. He pointed me in the right direction, and I eventually was in contact with a nationwide employee benefits consulting firm. My role was to recommend the general outline of a plan that would be reasonably adequate and at the same time would not be too expensive for the staff to pay into. The consulting firm did all the legal and actuarial work to make our plan both legal and financially sound. Since I was responsible for starting the retirement plan, I continued to manage it for a number of years, until we finally formed a benefits committee.

About the same time we were starting the retirement fund, Jim Downing and I concluded that The Navigators should voluntarily participate in the Social Security system. At that time, nonprofit organizations such as The Navigators had the option of participating or not. This has since changed. For Jim and me, the major issue was not the Social Security system as a retirement fund but the fact that only those in the system could benefit from Medicare at age sixty-five. We felt that not to participate would leave our staff exposed to the possibility of tremendous medical bills after age sixty-five when they were no longer on The Navigators' health-insurance plan.

Both of these decisions were unpopular at first. Apart from Jim Downing, the oldest Navigators were fifty-one or fifty-two, and most of us were in our thirties and forties. At that time people in their thirties and forties did not take retirement planning seriously. In fact, in The Navigator culture, the presumption was, "Navigators don't retire. They just continue working until they die." And the combination of contributing to the pension plan and Social Security necessitated the staff raising additional funds for their budgets. So with the attitude that Navigators don't retire and the cost to the individual's budget, these were not popular decisions. As I write these words, however, in 2012, all of our staff over sixty-five are now grateful that we implemented both the pension plan and participation in Social Security. And I suspect that our younger staff, a generation that is far more knowledgeable in these affairs than my generation, appreciates these plans also.

Of all that God enabled me to accomplish during those years, it was the start of the retirement plan and the decision to participate in Social Security and Medicare that give me the most satisfaction. That is because these initiatives clearly benefited the staff, though they were not popular at first.

Around 1970 several large charitable organizations were involved in some form of financial scandal. As a result there was a movement in Congress to more closely regulate nonprofit organizations. A Christian senator told two of the senior statesmen among Christian organizations that if Christian groups would begin to regulate themselves, he would try to head off legislative efforts.

As a result, letters were sent to a number of Christian organizations inviting them to send a representative to a meeting in Chicago to make plans to establish an umbrella group to help them keep their financial houses in order. Since I was treasurer of The Navigators, Lorne Sanny asked me to attend. It was decided that we would go ahead with such an organization, and a second meeting was scheduled. At that meeting I was selected to serve on the board of directors of what came to be known as the Evangelical Council for Financial Accountability, or ECFA.

At the second meeting seven standards of financial practice were established for all members of ECFA. A committee needed to be formed that would be responsible for assuring that all member organizations were complying with the standards. At the first meeting of the board I was asked to chair the standards committee, so from the very beginning of

ECFA I served on the board and also chaired the standards committee. I enjoyed these new responsibilities and also enjoyed getting to know many people from other organizations. I developed some deep friendships with some of them.

We were also able to make some significant changes in our property and liability insurance that have saved The Navigators thousands of dollars, but the details of this will come in the next chapter.

One of the most exciting things for me personally during this period was the writing of my first book, *The Pursuit of Holiness,* published in 1978. I mentioned in an earlier chapter that I had heard the statement that the Bible was given to guide our conduct and that I had prayed, "God, starting tonight, would You use the Bible to guide my conduct?" That was the actual seed of the book on holiness.

Because of the mistakes I had made and particularly, having gotten so deeply involved in the "just let Jesus live His life through you" theology, I was eager to help other people avoid the pitfalls I had experienced and for others who were involved in that theology to see the fallacy, so I was publicly teaching on the principle of dependent responsibility every opportunity I had.

In 1975 The Navigators started a publishing division called NavPress. Prior to that we had simply a materials department, which was responsible for shipping our Bible study and Scripture memory resources. But The Navigators decided that we should get into the book publishing ministry. At the time it was thought that this would give staff an opportunity to publish. As it turned out, very few members of our staff were oriented to writing books, so this goal was never fully realized. However, it was God's open door for me.

When NavPress started they had only one or two books to publish, so they went to the Glen Eyrie Conference Center message archives, which contained hundreds of messages given over a twenty-year period. They selected about a dozen messages and had them transcribed into printed form and distributed them as pocket-sized booklets. The most well known of these are Dawson Trotman's *Born to Reproduce* and Lorne Sanny's *How to Spend a Day in Prayer*. They selected two of my messages, which I think got a small distribution.

However, LeRoy Eims, one of our senior staff, who had written two or three books, read one of my booklets. One day we *just happened* to meet in the parking lot, and he said to me, "Your message has got a real bite to it. You ought to try your hand at writing." This challenge stuck in my mind. I had the message "The Pursuit of Holiness," which I had given from time to time for almost ten years, and now I had the challenge to put it into print.

I went to the editor of NavPress, who was a casual friend, and told him about my idea for a book. He replied, "It sounds good. Write a couple of chapters and let me take a look at it." That was all. Today, if anyone wants to publish with NavPress, there is a lengthy proposal they must work through even to get their foot in the door.

So I started writing in September 1976. Since our children were young and I had a full-time job at The Navigators office, I could only spend a few hours a week working on this project. I took the entire summer of 1977 off from writing in order to spend more time with the children. I picked up the writing again in September 1977 and finished in early 1978. The book was finally published and released in October of that year.

Shortly after the release of *The Pursuit of Holiness,* the pastor of a large evangelical church in our community asked if I would teach the book for ten weeks as one of their Wednesday night electives. I was delighted to have this opportunity. Preparing a lesson for each week caused me to have to reread the book carefully. As I did so, toward the end of the ten weeks the thought came to my mind, "There is not enough gospel in this book."

I thought that, based on my own experience (see chapter 10), when people take the pursuit of holiness seriously they will soon begin to see sin in their lives that they were unaware of or unconcerned about. This can cause a deepening sense of guilt if they do not know how to take that sin to the cross in repentance and faith in the work of Christ. So the last evening of the ten sessions I titled my lesson "The Chapter I Wish I Had Written." It was a lesson about the necessity of Christians to live by the gospel instead of by performance. It was the lesson I had learned for myself in Europe but at that time failed to realize every believer needs it. This eventually became a major theme of my ministry, though it took several years for me to develop the integration of living by the gospel and the pursuit of holiness.

As treasurer of The Navigators I was concerned that NavPress not lose any money on my book, so I was hoping they would sell at least five thousand copies. Much to everyone's surprise, they sold over five thousand copies in the first six weeks. From that point on, the sales continued to increase until in the early 1980s it made the best-seller list for paperbacks three years in a row, and it continues to sell well now thirty-five years after its original publication.

The wide distribution of *The Pursuit of Holiness* brought my name to the attention of many pastors and Christian leaders outside of The Navigators, so I began to get invitations to speak in churches and at weekend conferences. Those speaking engage-ments and the wide reception of the book had a synergistic effect, and soon my name became known in the wider Christian community.

I assumed *The Pursuit of Holiness* would be the only book I would write. After all, I did not consider myself a writer and felt that I had said all I wanted to say in *The Pursuit of Holiness*. But God had other plans, and we will see the unfolding of those plans in the next chapter.

CHAPTER 13

Transition Era

The period 1984–1994 was difficult for me. There were significant issues at work. By far, however, the most painful event of the ten years was the death of my beloved Eleanor, the one God had given me in fulfillment of Psalm 116:7. Eleanor had been a healthy person all of our married life. She was never sick and was in the hospital only twice, to deliver Kathy and Dan. On her birthday, June 19, 1987, she went to the doctor for what we assumed was a routine visit. Instead, the doctor discovered a large malignant tumor in her abdominal area. He assured us that her form of cancer responded readily to treatment. After seven weeks of radiation, the tumor had shrunk completely and the doctor was pleased.

On December 3, the day before my birthday, she noticed an enlarged lymph gland on her neck. Sure enough, cancer had spread to the lymph system but in a more aggressive form. The only treatment now would be chemotherapy, but for some reason Eleanor could not tolerate the chemo. Her doctor said to me one day, "I am in a difficult place. If I give her the chemo she needs, it will kill her. If I don't give her what she needs, the cancer will kill her." In June 1988 a consulting doctor noticed that Eleanor was having difficulty answering some of his questions. He suspected the cancer had spread to her brain, and that turned out to be true. From that time on she became more and more disoriented until she was no longer herself. She finally died November 9, 1988, just three weeks after our twenty-fifth wedding anniversary. Kathy had just graduated from college in May and Dan was a junior.

Back in September 1971, just after we moved to a somewhat larger house, The Navigators staff had a two-day retreat for all staff and spouses. Kathy had just started kindergarten, and Dan was almost four years old. We needed someone to stay with them for two nights. Jane Mollet, a Navigator contact from Missouri, had just moved to town to live with one of our executive secretaries. This lady recommended Jane to us as someone who could stay with the children.

We invited Jane to dinner to get mutually acquainted and especially for her to get to know the children. She agreed to stay with them for the two days and they had a ball. The kids loved her, so we continued to stay in contact with Jane. She was a dental hygienist and in a few years went to Niger, Africa, to work in a missionary dental clinic. The mission she was with closed that clinic for political reasons after Jane had been there only two years, so she returned to Colorado Springs to work. We kept in casual contact. As the years went by, she decided she did not want to remain a dental hygienist until retirement, so she moved to Denver to study interior design. That is where she lived when Eleanor died.

During the difficult days of 1988, when Eleanor was slowly dying, I thought God impressed on my mind the familiar promise from Jeremiah 29:11, "For I know the plans I have for you, declares the LORD, plans for welfare and not for evil, to give you a future and a hope." The impression was so strong that I felt it was a sin not to believe it. At the same time I had difficulty reconciling the promise with what was happening because I assumed the promise meant Eleanor would recover. When she eventually died, I was devastated and concluded God had not actually given me the promise.

I assumed I would be single the rest of my life. But then I received a condolence card from Jane in which she had written out the text of Jeremiah 29:11. At first I was irritated to have this verse brought up to me again, but then I began to wonder if perhaps she might be a part of God's fulfillment of the promise. I began to pursue this thought, and to make a long story short, we were married November 24, 1989.

Now, back to the issues at work. By 1979 the job of both corporate secretary and treasurer had grown too big for one person to handle. At my recommendation we hired a younger man to become treasurer.

The period from 1979 until the fall of 1984 was essentially uneventful at the office. It was during this time, however, that I wrote my second book, *The Practice of Godliness*. As mentioned earlier, I assumed *The Pursuit of Holiness* was the only book I would ever write, but around 1980, as I was reading Ephesians 4:22-24, I saw that growth in Christian character consisted not only in putting off sinful traits but also in putting on Christlike character. I decided I needed to write a second book setting forth the importance of putting on His character. This book was published in 1983.

In October 1984 things began to change for me in the office. One Thursday afternoon I was told that immediately I would be reporting to the treasurer, a man twenty years younger than I whom I had recommended that we hire back in 1979. No explanation was given and I asked for none.

I was stunned, confused, and humiliated. What had I done? Where had I failed? This news also came at a difficult time. I was scheduled to speak at a weekend conference beginning Friday night at a local church, and I was concerned that I would be too emotionally distraught to do an effective job.

But God came to my rescue. Friday morning I awakened with Job 1:21 going through my mind: "And he said, 'Naked I came from my mother's womb, and naked shall I return. The LORD gave, and the LORD has taken away; blessed be the name of the LORD.'" I knelt at our living-room couch and prayed, "Father, You gave and You have taken away. Blessed be Your name." I rose from that prayer at perfect peace about what had taken place and went to the conference that night as if nothing had happened. Obviously, such a dramatic change in my heart and the perfect peace I experienced could only happen as a result of the Holy Spirit's work.

A month later the headquarters leadership team was downsized, and I was one of those dropped from the team. But at that time, the U.S. director said to me, "I want you to hire an assistant so you will have more time for ministry." He had more insight into what God was doing than I did, but I did not appreciate it at the time. But the fact was, God was giving me more and more opportunities to teach the Bible on topics that I had lived out in daily experience. From 1985 onward, I had about fifteen speaking or teaching engagements each year. Finally in 1994, which was the worst year of my time in the office, I had an unbelievable twenty-eight speaking engagements. I would leave Friday morning for the engagement, return late Sunday night, and be back in my office Monday morning. The only way I could have done that was due to the decreased responsibility at headquarters.

During that time I also wrote four books:

True Fellowship (1985) is a study on the various ways *koinonia* (usually translated as fellowship) is used in the New Testament. It was a fascinating study, and I concluded that most Christians, including myself, knew very little of the riches in that one word *koinonia* as it is used in the New Testament.

Trusting God Even When Life Hurts (1988) is a study on the sovereignty, wisdom, and love of God as those three attributes are brought to bear on the difficult times in our lives. This book has been well received and widely used by Christian counselors. I have been deeply humbled by the number of people who have written or told me personally how much the book helped them through a difficult period.

Transforming Grace (1991) grew out of the seed that was sown back in 1979 when I taught the ten-week course on *The Pursuit of Holiness* and titled my last class "The Chapter I Wish I Had Written." It took ten years before I was ready to enlarge on that subject. The primary message of the book is that we are not only saved by grace but we should live by grace every day of our lives. So I wrote *Transforming Grace* to help us all understand what it means to live by grace instead of by works.

The Discipline of Grace (1994) was written in response to people who thought that in *Transforming Grace* I had undermined the strong challenge to holiness in *The Pursuit of Holiness*. The truth is each book had a different objective. We need the message of both books because it is only as we understand that God's acceptance of us is based on grace can we respond to a challenge to pursue holiness without falling into a performance mindset. So I wrote *The Discipline of Grace* to show that grace and discipline are not opposed to each other but in fact complement one another.

All these books were written outside of office hours, but I'm sure that no longer being involved in the leadership team gave me the reserve I needed to pour myself into these books.

Meanwhile, at the office the situation continued to go downhill, and I felt more and more marginalized. Lorne Sanny, by now retired, said to me one day, "You have been marginalized, haven't you?" The final blow to my morale came at the beginning of 1994 when my administrative assistant and I were moved to a temporary location six or seven miles away. Now I was no longer marginalized but isolated from other relationships in the office.

Fortunately, I never knew who was responsible for the increased marginalization, and it really doesn't matter, because ultimately it was God. No one can act apart from His will, as Lamentations 3:37 says: "Who has spoken and it came to pass, unless the Lord has commanded it?" God had a purpose in all of this, and He was at work.

It is foolhardy to speculate on why God orchestrates or allows certain things to happen. But I know two things it did for me. First, I was humbled, and to be humbled, though usually painful, is always good for us. Second, I was weaned from any emotional attachment to the headquarters environment where I had given thirty years of my life.

When a gardener wants to move a bush to another location, the first thing he does is cut around the entire bush with a sharp spade to cut the immediate soil around the bush from its larger surroundings. In the process of digging the spade into the ground the gardener will invariably cut off the ends of many roots. If roots had feelings, that would be painful. But the bush must be separated from its surroundings. I know now that God was in the process of moving me to another place in His garden. In order to do that, He had to, as it were, dig around me and emotionally separate me from the headquarters environment, but it was still painful.

Eleanor, the children, and I lived in one house for twenty years. We moved in the day Kathy started kindergarten, and though Eleanor had died, I was still living there when Dan graduated from college. After Jane and I were married, we knew we should move to another house. The day we moved I shed tears because of all the fond memories of twenty years I was leaving behind. By contrast, the day I left headquarters the last time, I did not shed a tear. Why? Because God had dug around me with the spade of His providence and had emotionally separated me from the administrative environment.

Looking back now, almost twenty years later, I think God was doing something even more important than emotionally separating me from the headquarters environment. Jesus said in John 12:24, "Unless a grain of wheat falls into the earth and dies, it remains alone; but if it dies, it bears much fruit." God had more fruitfulness in mind for me (though I did not know it), but in order to experience it I had some dying to do, and all the marginalization and isolation I experienced was part of the dying process. I had to die to being a part of the leadership at The Navigators headquarters. I had to die to my title, vice president for corporate affairs. I had to die to recognition for any accomplishments in the 1969–1979 years. But Jesus said, in effect, if we die we will bring forth fruit.

In sharing this painful period of my life I do not want to appear critical of The Navigators organization, nor of anyone who could have been involved. As an organization, The Navigators has been very good to me, and I continue to enjoy the respect of all the staff, including those who might have been a part of the leadership team at that time. It is clear to me that God was orchestrating those painful circumstances to prepare me for the next phase of life and ministry.

There was one bright spot during those years, and that was the founding of Stewardship Insurance Company. Back in the mid-1980s, I was consistently having difficulty getting an annual renewal for our property and liability insurance. A friend in another Christian organization gave me the name of an insurance broker in California that they were using. I contacted this man, and he was able to quickly renew our coverage for the next year. But after working with us a couple of years, he said to me and the friend at the other organization, "You folks should form your own captive insurance company."

Without going into the details, a captive insurance company is a form of self-insurance administered by a regular insurance company with an insured backup in case of catastrophic losses. The concept is used by all major corporations. A minimum amount of capital is required, so our broker suggested that we invite several other organizations to partner with us and form a multi-owner captive. So in 1990 we founded Stewardship Insurance Company. Not only did that solve our annual renewal problem, but in the first ten years The Navigators had saved over a million dollars. I served on the board of directors for Stewardship from its founding until I left Navigators headquarters at the end of 1994. God in His gracious provision provided this one fulfilling project for me to work on during those otherwise difficult years.

In 1993 I decided I wanted to leave The Navigators

headquarters when I turned sixty-five the following year. As my last days at the office were finally approaching, my administrative assistant told me she was planning a farewell party. Because of my marginalization and isolation I expected only a few close friends to come. Instead, almost the entire office staff turned out to give me a warm send-off. The executive director of ECFA came all the way from Washington, DC, and the broker who had "fathered" Stewardship Insurance Company came from San Francisco. Obviously, I was deeply touched. It was a very encouraging time after the earlier difficult years.

So in January 1995 I began the next phase of my journey with God. We will see what that looked like in the next chapter.

CHAPTER 14

Fruitful Ministry

The year 1995 was the beginning of fifteen years of fruitful ministry, but the year did not begin well at all. It was another lesson in the sovereignty and goodness of God.

The occasion was a study trip to Israel, something that had been on my desire list for many years. The tour group was to assemble in Atlanta for a flight to Tel Aviv. To assure that Jane and I did not miss that flight, I scheduled four hours in Atlanta before the tour group was to depart.

However, the plane from Denver to Atlanta had mechanical problems, not once but twice. I could see our four hours in Atlanta evaporating, so I tried to get seats on another airline. Nothing was available that would get us there in time. During this time, two Scripture verses came to my mind. The first was Ecclesiastes 7:13: "Consider the work of God: who can make straight what he has made crooked?" Through that verse God seemed to be saying, "I have made your way crooked; that is, I have blocked your plans and, try as you will, you cannot make it straight." But at the same time words from a second verse came to my mind: "I will never leave you nor forsake you" (Hebrews 13:5). It seemed as if God was saying to me through those Scriptures, "I am blocking your plans, but don't fear, because 'I will never leave you nor forsake you.'"

We did get to the departure gate in Atlanta, but they had already closed the door and would not allow us to board. One problem with missing an overseas flight is that there is usually only one flight a day, so if you miss a flight you wait twenty-four hours for the next one. This meant that we would miss the first day of our tour, but to me the greater problem was that there would be no one to meet us in Tel Aviv. I sent a message to the tour coordinator through Delta Airlines, but I had no assurance the message would get through to him. We finally arrived in Tel Aviv twenty-four hours later, not knowing what to expect but leaning on God's promise that He would not forsake us. We went through immigration and customs and exited the arrival hall. That exit took us directly onto the street outside. At least a couple hundred people were packed around the exit waiting to greet passengers.

I was anxious. What do we do now? About that time Jane, who has eagle eyes, said, "Look straight ahead." Standing there was a man holding a paper that said, "Mr. and Mrs. Bridges." What a relief! I choke up now, many years later, as I think of how God fulfilled His promise. "I will never leave you nor forsake you." The man and a partner put us into a Volkswagen van and drove us about four hours into the desert, where we caught up with our tour group around midnight.

I had memorized both Ecclesiastes 7:13 and Hebrews 13:5 years before. Intellectually I believed both of them, but on this occasion God wanted to drive home to my heart the reality of those Scriptures, and to do that I had to experience them. I learned two valuable lessons. First, we cannot maneuver around the sovereign will of God, regardless of what devices we resort to. Second, even when God makes our way crooked, He is with us every moment and He will not forsake us.

The remainder of 1995 was a time of fulfillment in ministry and, I trust, profitable for the kingdom of God. In addition to a number of teaching engagements in the States, Jane and I spent a month in Australia at the invitation of several churches. During that time we formed some deep friendships that we still cherish today. Jane is a remarkable woman in the way she can develop friendships with other women whom she meets in our ministry. It is largely through her that these friendships with other couples are formed.

In 1996 I had my first opportunity to teach for a week at a seminary. Preparing to teach in an academic setting forced me to organize my material in a more disciplined fashion. At that time I titled my course "Grace and Discipline." It was directed to showing that we need both. We need to learn to live by grace every day of our lives. At the same time, we need to practice the basic spiritual disciplines which God uses to transform us into the image of Christ. I kept reminding my students, most of whom were already pastors, that the practice of these disciplines does not earn us favor with God. One performance-oriented pastor said, "You have turned my theology upside down." Keep in mind that I had to learn the relationship of grace and the disciplines the hard way through lots of trial and error. Now I am passionate about helping others through my mistakes.

There were three highlights in the year 1997. The first was our joining the collegiate ministry of The Navigators. When the collegiate director invited me, he said, "We want you to be a Bible teacher and a father figure to the students." So it has been an exciting fifteen or so years to be able to teach the Bible, mostly to our younger staff and our students.

The second highlight was being invited to teach my one-week course on grace and discipline at the Sovereign Grace Ministries Pastors' College. This was the first of a continuing annual engagement, and I have been with them every year since except for two. My seminary teaching also expanded as well as our overseas ministry.

A third highlight of 1997 was the publishing of the book entitled *The Joy of Fearing God*. Several years before, I had read a single sentence from a highly respected theologian: "The fear of God is the soul of godliness." Since I was vitally interested in godliness, I decided I needed to dig more deeply into the Bible's teaching on the fear of God. At the same time, I was approached by a friend, then president of another publishing company, about writing a book on the fear of God. Since I was already interested in the subject, I agreed to do so, and over a number of months, wrote the book. I consider it one of my better books on a subject that is largely overlooked but desperately needed among believers today. In fact, I said to Jane one day, "I need to reread this book once a month myself," not because of my writing but because of the importance of the subject.

The years 1998 through 2009 were largely the same, with opportunities to teach in several more seminaries and minister in more countries overseas.

However, one important change occurred in my teaching curriculum about the year 2000. I changed the name of the course from "Grace and Discipline" to something like "Gospel-Based Transformation," and I began to use the word *gospel* more than *grace* in my teaching. One reason for this change was that I felt the word grace was being misunderstood as meaning that God overlooks the minor sins in our lives.

The most important reason, however, was that people were looking at the concept of grace by itself without realizing that God's grace can only come to us through Jesus Christ and as a result of His sinless life and death on the cross for our sins. To say it succinctly, without the gospel there is no grace. Here I should clarify the word *gospel*. Technically, the gospel is a message about the work of Christ, but I use it as a shorthand expression for all that Christ did in His life and death and the fruit resulting from that. Believers need to learn to find their acceptance with God in the work of Christ rather than what has become an abstract concept of grace. That is why I made the change.

Several years before, I had read what I now consider the most important book I've ever read. It is a dense five-hundred-page book written in nineteenth-century prose.

Its title is *The Apostles' Doctrine of Atonement*, written by Scottish theologian George Smeaton. In this book Smeaton looks at every verse on the atonement from Acts to Revelation, so it is very thorough. To me, though, the value of the book lies in his continued emphasis on what I call the representative union of Christ with His people.

In chapter 9 I recount how I had come to an understanding of the believer's union with Christ as taught by Jesus in His analogy of the vine and the branches in John 15. I call this the living union through which Christ imparts His life to us. But there is another aspect of our union with Christ that I call our representative union. This means that all that Christ did in His life of perfect obedience, as well as His death on the cross, He did as our representative and substitute. We need both His death and His perfect obedience to make us righteous before an infinitely holy God. So Smeaton would over and over again say something like, "When Christ lived a perfectly obedient life, you lived a perfectly obedient life. When Christ died on the cross, you died on the cross."

This twofold nature of Christ's work is brought out succinctly in 2 Corinthians 5:21: "For our sake he made him to be sin who knew no sin, so that in him we might become the righteousness of God." This verse is often called "The Great Exchange," that is, God took all our sin and charged it to Christ. Then He took the perfect righteousness of Christ and credited that to us. This is why Paul said in Philippians 3:9, "And be found in him, not having a righteousness of my own that comes from the law, but that which comes through faith in Christ, the righteousness from God that depends on faith."

This means our daily relationship with God is always based on the complete and finished work of Christ, never our own performance. I found this truth almost a revolutionary concept for many people. To use an analogy, it was like exchanging an old black-and-white television set for one of the latest high-tech color models. I greatly enjoyed teaching this dual aspect of the gospel and our representative union with Christ. However, I also felt my primary calling in both teaching and writing was to call God's people to a serious pursuit of holiness. By now my first book, *The Pursuit of Holiness*, had sold well over a million copies, and I believed that God had so blessed this book because it is indeed a serious call to holiness.

So where does the gospel fit into a ministry of challenge to the pursuit of holiness? The answer is that the gospel, rightly understood and applied to one's daily life, is the only true and lasting motivation for the pursuit of holiness. It is the gospel that changes "I ought to obey God" to "I want to obey" out of gratitude for what He has done for me through Christ. (For a more complete treatment of this subject, see my book *The Transforming Power of the Gospel*, NavPress, 2012.)

During this period I also wrote three more books:

- *The Gospel for Real Life*, 2002
- *Growing Your Faith*, 2004
- *Respectable Sins*, 2007

I also coauthored two books with my friend Bob Bevington:

- *The Great Exchange*, 2007 (based on Smeaton's book)
- *The Bookends of the Christian Life*, 2009

So with all my opportunities to teach both in the States and overseas, plus the books written during that time, the years 1995 through 2011 were joyous and, I trust, fruitful years.

These were also years of public recognition. In 2005 I was awarded an honorary Doctor of Divinity degree from Westminster Theological Seminary. Then I was one of several Navigator staff who received a Lifetime Influencer Award from the U.S. Navigators at their national staff conference in November 2011. But during those years the greatest satisfaction I experienced was the testimonies of people whose lives had been deeply influenced by one of the books I had written. When we go to be with God, it is not the awards or recognition we have received, but the lives impacted for Christ that will count when each of us hopes to hear, "Well done, good and faithful servant" (Matthew 25:21).

Recently I have been reflecting on those years of unusual fruitfulness. The thought has come to me that, as far as this life is concerned, this was the destination that God had in mind when at age seventeen it seemed that He took me by the hand and said, "Come with me." God planned for me to be a Christian writer and teacher, but why did He wait until I was sixty-five to bring this to full development? I believe the reason is that He wanted me to write and teach truths that have to be learned through lots of difficult experiences and lots of mistakes. But by His providence He has been leading me all the way. To Him be the glory!

But a schedule such as I kept for over fifteen years could not continue indefinitely, so God had to slow it down, and in the next chapter we will see how He did it.

CHAPTER 15

A Time of Reflection

Through the first eighty years of my life God gave me amazingly good health and physical stamina. But in 2010 conditions began to change. Both my vision and hearing in my left ear began to decline, and the effects of my spinal deformity at birth started to more and more affect my ability to walk and to stand.

It was not until 2012, however, that my health really took a turn for the worse. I finally had to have surgery to repair two valves in my heart. At first, because I did not have any blocked arteries, the surgeon planned to do a minimally invasive procedure through an opening in the side. I was delighted with this prospect because it entails a much shorter recovery time. But a CAT scan of my chest revealed the deformity in my breastbone that I had had from birth. That deformity would prevent the surgeon from doing the surgery from the side and necessitated his opening up my sternum (breastbone) to get to the heart. This of course was major surgery.

Naturally I was disappointed at this news, but as I left the doctor's office Psalm 139:13 again came to my mind:

"For you formed my inward parts; you knitted me together in my mother's womb." God had created me with that deformity in my mother's womb, and that was part of His plan for my life eighty-two years after I was born. Once again I had to believe that God's plan was better than one I would have desired.

The surgery actually went very well, and I expected to start the recovery process in two or three weeks. But again God had other plans. Some complications arose soon after surgery, and I saw no progress at all for about a month. I began to wonder if one aspect of the complications would ever change, and so again I had to wrestle with Ecclesiastes 7:13: "Who can make straight what he has made crooked?"

I also had to go back to Hebrews 13:5: "I will never leave you nor forsake you." Though the absolute sovereignty of God over our lives is consistently taught throughout Scripture, it is not the uncaring sovereignty of a despot but of a God who is just as loving and caring as He is sovereign. But we have to by faith believe that truth when His ways are different from that which we desire.

My health issues have been minor compared to what many people experience, and I do not want to belabor them any more than will serve the purpose of illustrating that we never graduate from God's school of adversity and faith. We will be walking by faith until we die. As the writer of Hebrews said of some of the Old Testament saints, "All these people were still living by faith when they died" (11:13, NIV). But this health brief will also show how God slowed me down from the busy schedule I had kept for years.

Actually the years 2010 and 2011 were not unproductive. I wrote three books during that period, all of which were published in 2012.

The first, titled *The Transforming Power of the Gospel,* is a condensed version of the one-week course I had been teaching in various schools and seminaries over the years. This book shows clearly the relationship between the gospel and Christian growth.

The second, titled *Who Am I?,* is a short book on our identity in Christ. It was written to help people find their identity in Christ and His work for them, rather than in their own or other people's appraisal of them.

The third book, *True Community,* is a major revision of my 1985 book, *True Fellowship.* The concept of community has in recent years become an important one, both in the church and in parts of the secular culture. The various applications to life of the Greek word *koinonia,* however, actually form the basis of authentic community. This is why NavPress and I agreed to revise *True Fellowship* to make it more relevant to today's culture.

I have titled this chapter "A Time of Reflection," and that is what the remainder of the chapter is about. First I want to do a time of reflection on the seven most important spiritual lessons I have learned in over sixty years as a Christian. Then I will share some reflections on the notable demonstrations of the providence of God in my life.

SPIRITUAL LESSONS

I have learned many lessons over my sixty-plus years of being a believer, but these are seven that stand out to me. Each one of the seven has made a significant change in the way I view the Christian life and how to live it. Some of the lessons may seem self-evident, but when I became a Christian at age eighteen, despite having grown up in church, I was essentially biblically illiterate. Here are the seven lessons:

Lesson One: The Bible is meant to be applied to specific life situations. This includes both God's commands to be obeyed and His promises to be relied upon. Here, of course, is where Scripture memorization is so valuable. The Holy Spirit can bring to our minds specific Scriptures to apply to specific situations.

Lesson Two: All who trust in Christ as Savior are united to Him in a living way just as the branches are united to the vine (see John 15:1-5). This means that as we abide in Him — that is, depend on Him in faith — His very life will flow into and through us to enable us to be fruitful both in our own character and our ministry to others.

Lesson Three: The pursuit of holiness and godly character is neither by self-effort nor simply letting Christ "live His life through you." Rather, it does involve our most diligent efforts but with a recognition that we are dependent on the Holy Spirit to enable us and to bless those efforts. I call this "dependent responsibility."

Lesson Four: The sudden understanding of the

doctrine of election was a watershed event for me that significantly affected my entire Christian life. For example, it was the realization of God's sovereignty in election that led me to study further the sovereignty of God in all of life. It also produced a deep sense of gratitude and, I trust, humility, of realizing salvation was entirely of Him.

Lesson Five: The representative union of Christ and the believer means that all that Christ did in both His perfect obedience and His death for our sins is credited to us. Or to say it another way, because Christ is our representative before the Father, it was just of God to charge our sins to Christ and to credit His righteousness to us. So we as believers stand before God perfectly cleansed from both the guilt and defilement of our sin, but also clothed in the perfect righteousness of Christ.

Lesson Six: The gospel is not just for unbelievers in their coming to Christ. Rather, all of us who are believers need the gospel every day because we are still practicing sinners. The gospel, embraced every day, helps keep us from self-righteousness because it frees us to see our sin for what it really is. Also, gratitude for what God has done for us in Christ should motivate us to want to pursue godly character and to offer ourselves as living sacrifices to Him.

Lesson Seven: We are dependent on the Holy Spirit to apply the life of Christ to our lives. Someone has said (and this is a paraphrase), God the Father purposes, Christ accomplishes what the Father has purposed, and the Holy Spirit applies to our lives what Christ accomplished. To do this, the Spirit works in us directly and He also enables us to work. All the spiritual strength that we need comes to us from Christ through the Holy Spirit.

THE PROVIDENCE OF GOD

Actually, the providence of God is active every moment of our lives, but there are times when the action of God particularly stands out, bringing about some major changes in our lives. These changes may be for good or bad as we evaluate them, but for the believer God has promised to redeem even the so-called bad ones because He causes all events in our lives — the good and the bad, the big and the little — to work together for our good, that is, to conform us to the likeness of Christ (see Romans 8:28-29).

Some significant acts of God's providence in my life have been recounted throughout the previous chapters. But in order that you might see the thread of these acts of God throughout my life, I want to briefly review them.

- The four physical defects I was born with: cross-eyed, totally deaf in right ear, and deformities in my spine and breastbone. Through them I came to appreciate Psalm 139:13 and have had to resort to it many times. Through Psalm 139:16, I also came to accept the fact that the many negative circumstances of my early years were ordained of God before I was born and were part of His plan for my overall life. (chapter 2)
- A poor algebra teacher in ninth grade resulted

several years later in changing my major to general engineering, which included a lot of business courses. (chapter 4)

- In February 1947, I just *happened* to see the article in our local newspaper about the new navy college program for training officers. It is important to realize that my college education came through the navy, because several years later while on active duty as a navy officer, I came in contact with The Navigators. (chapter 5)

- A few weeks later I managed to pass the navy hearing test, despite my "slight loss of hearing in right ear." (chapter 5)

- In August 1948, my brother invited me to go with him on a home visit. That night I admitted to myself I was not a Christian and asked Christ to be my Savior. (chapter 6)

- September 1948, just one week after trusting Christ, the thought came into my mind, "Now that you really are a Christian, you need to start reading the Bible." (chapter 6)

- The summer of 1950, I met a sailor who urged me to write to The Navigators for their Topical Memory System. (chapter 6)

- In December 1951, I went to a Christian meeting and met another navy officer who had shortly before come in contact with The Navigators. That encounter did not result in anything, but the next week his ship and my ship sent us to seminars on shore and we were in adjoining classrooms. We just *happened* to meet again, and this time he directed me to a meeting at The Navigators. (chapter 7)

- In January 1952, at a Navigators' Bible study, the leader said, "The Bible was not given to increase your knowledge but to guide your conduct." Though that is not a good statement, the Holy Spirit used it to help me see that the Bible was meant to be applied to one's daily life. That was the seed that resulted in the book *The Pursuit of Holiness* in 1978. (chapter 7)

- In the fall of 1952 while doing Bible study, I had a vague sense that God might be calling me to serve with The Navigators. (chapter 7)

- On December 26, 1952, I failed a hearing test and as a result was given a medical discharge in July 1953. I moved into The Navigators' representative's home as a trainee. (chapter 7)

- In the fall of 1953, I was hired by Convair Aircraft, but as a technical writer instead of an engineer. This turned out to be a part of God's preparation for my writing years later, because I had to learn to write clearly and simply, now a recognized characteristic of my books. (chapter 8)

- In the spring of 1955, I wondered if I should use my veteran's educational benefits to attend seminary. The catalogues I sent for didn't create any desire to go to seminary. That was God's way of closing that door and keeping me in The Navigators. (chapter 8)

- In June 1955, I was invited to work in the office at The Navigators headquarters, now in Colorado Springs, Colorado. That was the beginning of almost forty years of service in various administrative roles in The Navigators. (chapter 9)
- In the fall of 1955, I had an increasingly strong impression that I should terminate a romantic relationship I had started earlier that year. (chapter 9)
- In March 1957, I had another strong impression from Psalm 116:7, "Return, O my soul, to your rest; for the LORD has dealt bountifully with you," that God was promising to give me a wife. The impression was so strong that I wrote the date, March 17, 1957, in the margin of my Bible. (chapter 9)
- In the fall of 1959, I was given a scholarship to the Dale Carnegie Public Speaking Course. This was the foundation for all the speaking and teaching I would be doing in the next fifty years. (chapter 9)
- In November 1959, I had the strong impression I should write a letter of thanks to my dad, which I did. He had two massive heart attacks in the next weeks and died December 21, 1959, without my ever having a chance to talk with him. (chapter 9)
- In December 1959, I was asked to go to Europe to be the administrative assistant to the Europe director, thus keeping me in administration, but with a different perspective. (chapter 9)

- In January 1960, I read a booklet, *The Doctrine of Election*. I considered it heresy, but the next day the Holy Spirit worked in my mind in such a way that I immediately embraced the doctrine I had scorned the day before. (chapter 10)
- I arrived in Holland in March 1960. The first weekend I was asked to fill in for the planned speaker at a one-day conference. This was my first time to speak to an audience of more than a dozen, and it was God's first step in my ultimately teaching the Bible on a full-time basis. (chapter 10)
- In March 1963, there was the unusual circumstance of my having dinner with Eleanor Miller on the anniversary of the day I sensed God had given me a promise from Psalm 116:7 about marriage. We were married seven months later. (chapter 10)
- There was the honorarium check from my brother's church that was almost exactly the price of a round-trip ticket to meet Eleanor once again at her parents' home in Pittsburgh. (chapter 11)
- In 1964, there was the move to Kansas City and then the move back to The Navigators headquarters in 1965 to manage the office. This kept me in administration rather than allowing me to fail in an area ministry. (chapter 11)
- In 1969, I was appointed as corporate secretary and treasurer. This was the beginning of ten years of significant contribution to The Navigators administration. (chapter 12)

- The founding of the Evangelical Council for Financial Accountability (ECFA) and my service on its board of directors and as chairman of the standards committee. (chapter 12)

- In 1978, the publication of my first book, *The Pursuit of Holiness,* and the exposure to the wider Christian community resulting from that. (chapter 12)

- In January 1979, the teaching of a ten-week course on *The Pursuit of Holiness,* which caused me to realize the importance of the gospel in a challenge to holiness. This opened a whole new door of thinking to me and greatly influenced my ministry from that time forward. (chapter 12)

- On November 9, 1988, the death of Eleanor. (chapter 13)

- On November 24, 1989, my marriage to Jane Mollet. (chapter 13)

- The day in October 1984 when I was told I would immediately report to the treasurer and how the Holy Spirit brought to my mind Job 1:21: "And he said, 'Naked I came from my mother's womb, and naked shall I return. The LORD gave, and the LORD has taken away; blessed be the name of the LORD,'" which enabled me to accept the change. (chapter 13)

- A month later I was dropped off the U.S. Leadership Team and over time eventually marginalized and even geographically isolated for a year. (chapter 13)

- The U.S. director asked me to hire an assistant so I

could devote more time to ministry. (chapter 13)

- Through those difficult months God providentially severed me emotionally from The Navigators headquarters and also took me through a "dying process" to better prepare me for the ministry He had for me. (chapter 13)
- In 1995, the study tour to Israel and how I experienced the reality of two verses: Ecclesiastes 7:13 and Hebrews 13:5. Through that experience I learned it is futile to try to get around God's sovereign plans, but I also learned the reality of His promise that He will never leave us nor forsake us. (chapter 14)
- The seventeen years (1995–2011) of amazing fruitfulness in both teaching and writing and the more recent thought that, as far as this life is concerned, this was the destination God had in mind when, at age seventeen, it seemed He took me by the hand and said, "Come with me." (chapter 14)

The years 1955 through 2011 were a period of fifty-six years. I look at twenty-five of them as experiencing the blessing of God on my labors. Another fifteen years were clearly painful, and another sixteen were neither particularly painful nor blessed. As I look at those numbers I feel especially blessed by God. I think of relatives and friends whose lives seem to have been marked more by pain than anything else, and I realize how blessed I have been.

WHAT ABOUT THE FUTURE?

A few months after my heart surgery in April 2012, I asked my cardiologist if my heart would eventually return to the same efficiency it had when I was in my seventies. He said, no, so I mentally began to prepare for a "new normal" life and ministry, including a much reduced schedule.

Much to my surprise, it is not as different as I thought it would be. Physically I feel fine, although it does not take much exertion to get me breathing heavily. But I can tell no difference in my physical ability to speak and teach. In January 2013 I taught twenty hours over five days at a missionary training center with no unusual tiredness. Shortly after, I spoke eight times at a three-day weekend conference, and again I experienced no noticeable ill effects. So I am beginning to resume somewhat of an "old normal" schedule. I have no idea how long God will allow me to do this, or even want me to do it.

I do know that for over sixty-five years God has been leading me by His invisible hand of providence, most of the time in fairly routine ways and sometimes in remarkable ways. But whether it was routine or remarkable, God has been leading me. I trust Him to continue to do that until He calls me home.

Someone has said, "Everyone has a life story, but not every story gets written." I have written mine, not because my story is particularly important, but because it so clearly and so consistently over the years illustrates the unusual providence of God in the life of a very unpromising young boy. As you read this, I hope that you can see why I say, it seems that when I was seventeen years old, God took me by the hand and said, "Come with Me."

But what has been true of me is, in principle, true of every one of us who are His children. You may not feel as if God has taken you by the hand, but that is essentially what He has done. I know that many, many believers have little or no awareness of the truth of God's providence and consequently do not see God's "invisible hand" in their lives. It is my prayer that this book will serve to increase the awareness in many lives of God's providential working and will, through this, bring comfort to many people and greater glory to God.

GOD TOOK ME
by the HAND

Questions for Reflection,
Discussion, and Application

Chapter 1: Introduction

1. Jerry speaks here of how his eightieth birthday sparked "a lot of reflecting on God's working in my life." What events or occasions have generated the same kind of reflection in your own life?

2. Jerry adds that his life has included hard and discouraging times, "but through it all, I see God's hand drawing me along the path He ordained for me before I was born." What are some of the most important ways you've seen this kind of oversight from God upon your life?

3. God's providence — what Jerry describes as "the invisible hand of God" — is something that he says few people understand and appreciate. How would you summarize your personal understanding of God's "providence"?

4. Looking back on his youth, Jerry says he "certainly was not a candidate to be someone used by God." Would that statement also describe how you view your younger days?

What do you think is actually required in order to be a candidate for being used by God?

Chapter 2: An Unpromising Beginning

1. Compare the details in Jerry's childhood with the earliest experiences in your life. What is most different between his childhood story and yours, and what is most alike?

2. In relating the vocational and financial struggles of his father, Jerry states this principle: "God is as much in control of our bad decisions as He is our good ones." How easy is it for you to agree with that?

How do you see such a principle playing out in your life and in the lives of others you know?

3. Jerry brings in the words of David in verses 13 and 16 of Psalm 139. Review those verses and Jerry's explanation of them. What important perspectives do these verses give you regarding your background and your physical makeup?

   What trust and confidence in God do these truths provide for you?

   How do these truths affect your perspective on your future?

4. David's words in Psalm 40:13 are also mentioned by Jerry as applying to his life story. Which lines in that passage have the strongest bearing on your life story?

5. Jerry also quotes Jacob's self-perception as expressed in Genesis 32:10. How much do Jacob's words there match your own self-perception?

Chapter 3: The Biblical Foundation

1. In this chapter's opening paragraph, is there anything you would add to Jerry's definition of God's providence?

2. "Absolutely nothing can happen outside the controlling hand of God," Jerry states. How difficult is it for you to fully believe and accept this truth?

   How has your view of God's providence developed and changed over the years?

   Jerry cites a number of passages in support of his statement. Which of those passages are most helpful for you in thinking about this topic?

3. Jerry describes how God directs all events and circumstances so that they further His purposes. As you consider this, what would you say are the highest purposes that God is pursuing in our world today?

To the best of your understanding, what are God's highest purposes that He's pursuing in your life at this time?

How confident are you that God will indeed accomplish these purposes?

4. Jerry discusses how God's orchestration of events brings about the display of "the beauty of His glory." And yet we see much tragedy and evil in the world. In light of that, how are we to understand this higher "beauty"?

5. Review Jerry's comments on the story in Matthew 17 of Peter catching the fish with a coin in its mouth. Jerry goes on to relate how the expression "That was a God thing" can indicate our failure to adequately give God glory for the more ordinary ways He governs our lives. How do you respond to this suggestion?

Have you described something (or heard someone else describe it) as "a God thing"? What was the intended meaning?

Is there any event or circumstance in our lives that is *not* "a God thing"? Why or why not?

6. Review Jerry's explanation of God's "common grace." How do you most clearly see this grace at work in the world around you?

What evidences of God's common grace are you most grateful for?

7. As we receive instruction and guidance from the Holy Spirit through the Scriptures, why do we need to be cautiously aware that our perceptions are *not* infallible?

8. Jerry raises the question, "How does the Holy Spirit instruct and guide us?" How would you summarize the different parts of his answer to that question?

    How have you seen this process operating most recently in your life?

9. What value do you see in the two "tests" Jerry mentions for determining the validity of something we feel the Holy Spirit has spoken to us through His "inaudible voice"?

    How would you rank the importance of those two tests?

10. As we've seen, in this chapter Jerry explores many passages of Scripture to unfold the meaning of God's providence. Which passages mentioned here would you say are the most important for you to remember and keep in your heart?

Chapter 4: School Days

1. Compare the details of Jerry's school experiences with what those days were like in your life. What is most different between his education story and yours, and what is most alike?

2. Jerry also talks here about his first job experiences as a boy. What were the most life-shaping work experiences in your own childhood and teenage years?

3. What impresses you most in Jerry's description of his mother's death and his subsequent grief, and how does his experience compare with any similar situation in your life or in the lives of people close to you?

4. Jerry relates Deuteronomy 29:29 to his uncertainty about why God allowed him to continue playing football in high school. In your own past, what circumstances would you relate that same verse to?

5. As Jerry describes his repeated occurrences of "going forward" to secure his salvation, how do you compare his experiences with your own initial religious experiences?

    Jerry writes of "trying to convince myself that I must be a Christian." What similar attempts have marked your own life?

    He also states that any of us "can do all the right things and believe the right doctrine and still not be a genuine believer." In what ways have you seen this to be true?

Chapter 5: A New Beginning

1. The Old Testament stories of Ruth and Esther are mentioned here for their intriguing appeal and special meaning for Jerry. What do these stories have in common?

2. What gets your attention most in Jerry's description of how he transitioned from high school into the navy?

3. How do Jerry's experiences here demonstrate God's taking him "by the hand"?

4. Jerry refers readers to 1 Corinthians 1:27-29 in support of his thoughts here on how God often works in our lives. Look up this passage in your Bible. What are the central points Paul is making here?

How do these points relate most clearly to Jerry's situation at this time in his life?

How do these points relate most clearly to your current situation in life?

Chapter 6: College Days

1. What gets your attention most in Jerry's description of his days in college and naval training?

2. What aspects of God's care was Jerry experiencing when he finally became assured of his salvation?

3. Jerry points here to Romans 5:1 as a description of his experience. In what ways do the realities in that verse have meaning for your life?

4. Jerry recalls how he got started in reading the Bible regularly, more than six decades ago. Is Bible reading a consistent and highly valued practice in your life? If so, how did it begin?

5. God's sovereign will over our lives, Jerry says, does not make us merely His puppets. How would you express in your own words Jerry's explanation about this?

6. Compare Ezra 1:1 with God's words to Persia's King Cyrus in Isaiah 45:4. What do these verses illustrate about how God sometimes works?

Chapter 7: Naval Service

1. What gets your attention most in Jerry's description of his years in naval service?

2. Observing the goings-on of American sailors in foreign ports, Jerry says, "I soon realized that I did not have the spiritual stamina to live a Christian life in such an ungodly atmosphere." Why was this recognition so important?

   How would your own spiritual stamina hold up in that environment, or in something similar?

3. How did God work to overcome Jerry's lack of spiritual maturity in these days?

How has He worked to do the same in your life story?

4. How was Jerry growing in his understanding of the Bible's purpose in his life?

   How would you summarize your full understanding of the Bible's purpose in your life?

5. In the last part of this chapter, review the way Jerry summarizes what God accomplished in his life during his twenty-six months of active duty. How does this compare with what God has accomplished in your life as a foundation for your further spiritual growth?

Chapter 8: San Diego Navigator Home

1. Have you experienced something similar to Jerry's being disgruntled with God for not finding him a job more quickly?

What did you learn from that situation?

What did Jerry learn from his situation?

2. In your own words, summarize Jerry's explanation of how this situation illustrates God's providence.

3. The lessons that God drives home in our hearts most deeply often come, Jerry says, "through a combination of Scripture and providential circumstances." How have you seen this to be true in your own life?

How can you be better prepared to quickly learn such lessons in the future?

4. Why is it so wrong to complain against God? Isn't it healthy to "vent" our frustrations? What do you think about this?

What Scriptures do you know that are most relevant to this issue? How does God want us to understand it?

5.   During this time in Jerry's life, God was bringing him a wide variety of experiences that would prepare him for serving God in the future. How has He done something similar in your life?

6.   Near the end of this chapter, Jerry speaks of a restlessness that occurred at this time. How have you experienced something similar that led to a God-ordained change of circumstances for you?

Chapter 9: Glen Eyrie

1.   Jerry finds it "fascinating and encouraging to realize that God is directing the events of our lives to accomplish His overall purposes. This is true of every believer. It is just as true of you as it is of me." How fully do you share Jerry's fascination and encouragement over this truth?

2. Evaluate and summarize what Jerry learned at this time about his financial giving to God's work. How does this compare with lessons that God has taught you in this area?

3. Read in 1 Kings 17:8-16 the story Jerry mentions about Elijah and the widow. How does verse 16 apply to your life?

4. Jerry speaks here of his gaining a heart for world missions. How important should such a concern be for believers today?

   How important to you is a concern for world missions?

5. Psalm 116:7 brought special comfort to Jerry at this time. What meaning do you see in these words for your life?

6. Pointing us to Galatians 5:17, Jerry speaks of the conflict between the flesh and the Spirit and its affect on our Bible reading. How do you see this truth at work in your own Bible intake?

7. Jerry goes on to describe his coming to see that the "passive approach" to our sanctification is not biblical. Look carefully at how he describes his struggle over this issue. You may want to also carefully review chapters 6–8 in Romans, passages that were particularly helpful to Jerry at this time. What was most important in how Jerry reached his conclusion about the passive approach?

How would you summarize the principle of "dependent responsibility," which Jerry describes?

What is most important about this principle in how it relates to your life?

8. Describe in your own words what Jerry learned at this time about God's love for him and for others, and about his own responsibility to love.

   What are the major lessons that God has taught you in regard to loving others?

9. Describe also in your own words what Jerry was learning about the "living union" that believers share with Christ.

   What are the most important aspects of this truth that God has impressed upon you?

10. How does Jerry evidence here his understanding of how God has uniquely gifted him?

11. How do you continue to see God's hand at work in guiding Jerry during these years?

12. What was Jerry learning at this time about faith?

13. How would you describe what Jerry seems to be learning most during this period specifically about the *gospel* — the saving good news of Jesus Christ?

Chapter 10: Europe

1. What was Jerry learning at this time about the biblical doctrine of election? Summarize this in your own words.

Jerry points his readers to Ephesians 1:4. What exactly does this verse teach us about this doctrine?

2. God brought Romans 12:1 to Jerry's mind at this time. Jerry states that he was now able to "present" himself to God while understanding more deeply God's mercy and grace. Why is this important?

3. Jerry stresses here "the sovereignty of God in all things, including the salvation of sinners." As you review John 3:38, how would you explain in your own words how God's sovereignty is at work in a person's salvation?

   Look at Ephesians 2:1, which Jerry also refers to here. How would you explain the importance of the truth in that passage as it relates to our experience of salvation?

   Another passage Jerry points to here is Romans 10:13. How does Jerry relate God's free offer of salvation with the doctrine of election?

How do these various passages help in your own understanding of our salvation from God?

Why does Jerry place so much importance on his understanding of these matters as they relate to his life's story?

4. Jerry writes that "our experiences, as real as they may be, must always be validated by the Scriptures." Do you agree? Why or why not?

5. How was Jerry made more aware of God's holiness?

What impact did this have on his view of himself?

How does God's holiness relate to the way you view yourself?

6. Jerry mentions here his belief (explained more fully later) that Christians must "live by the gospel every day of our lives, even if we are not aware of any so-called 'major sins' in our lives." What does he appear to mean by this?

   How fully does this match your own convictions about the gospel?

7. What gets your attention most in Jerry's description of his years in Europe?

8. How do you continue to see God's hand at work in guiding Jerry during this time?

9. Jerry writes that as God leads us, "it is just as important that He keep us from the wrong ministry as that He directs us to the right one." To what extent have you witnessed the importance of this truth?

10. At a desperate time, the words of Isaiah 53:6 helped Jerry "live by the gospel." What specific help does this verse offer you in doing the same?

11. Summarize how God dealt with Jerry in his exploration of the doctrine of "sinless perfection."

    What is your own response and belief concerning this doctrine?

12. What gets your attention most in how Jerry describes the launch of his relationship with Eleanor Miller?

13. In this chapter's last paragraph, Jerry discusses the place of "dramatic encounters with God" in the way He works in our lives. What are Jerry's conclusions about this?

In the way God has led in your life, what place has there been for dramatic encounters with God?

14. From what you see in this chapter, what difference was the good news of Jesus actually making in Jerry's life at this time?

Chapter 11: Early Married Life

1. How do you most obviously see God's hand at work in guiding Jerry during these years?

2. What is Jerry continuing to learn here about his personal giftedness and the way God uses it?

What are the major lessons you've learned about your own particular giftedness, and the way God uses it?

3. How does Jerry emphasize here the importance of Scripture memory?

   What role has the discipline of Scripture memory played in your life?

4. Jerry also stresses that both God's commands *and* His promises are important for us to memorize and live by. How do you see this importance in your life?

5. Look at Jerry's answer to the question, "Doesn't the providence of God include times of failure?" How have you seen that question answered in your life?

6. Jerry says he "learned early on that most major changes result in criticism from some quarters." How have you seen this to be true?

What do you see as the best approaches for handling such criticism?

7. From what you see in this chapter, what difference was the good news of Jesus actually making in Jerry's life at this time?

Chapter 12: Secretary/Treasurer

1. Carefully look over Jerry's discussion of 1 Peter 4:11 and Isaiah 26:12. What conclusion does Jerry draw from these verses?

As you think about the spiritual dynamics represented in these biblical truths, how do they apply in your life at this time?

2. What gets your attention most in this chapter's narrative about this part of Jerry's administrative career with The Navigators?

What do you see as his major accomplishments in these years?

How do you most clearly see God's hand at work in guiding Jerry during these years?

3. What was Jerry continuing to learn about his personal giftedness?

4. What impresses you most about the unfolding of Jerry's ministry of writing books?

5. Jerry describes how he came to realize that there was "not enough gospel" in his first book, *The Pursuit of Holiness*. Describe in your own words what he means by this.

6. From what you see in this chapter, what difference was the good news of Jesus actually making in Jerry's life at this time?

Chapter 13: Transition Era

1. What impresses you most in Jerry's descriptions of these years of transition?

2. In Jerry's experience here of God's providence and guidance, key roles are played by God's words in Jeremiah 29:11 and the words of Job in Job 1:21. What perspective do these Scriptures give you as you continue to look to God for His care and guidance?

3. What common patterns do you see in the themes and topics of the books that Jerry was writing during this time?

4. Jerry speaks of how his office situation "continued to go downhill, and I felt more and more marginalized." How did he respond to this situation?

    In the face of this difficulty, what were the most important truths Jerry understood about God's purposes for his life?

5. Look at the words of Jesus in John 12:24. How does Jerry bring the truth of this passage into his own work experiences at this time?

    How do these words of Jesus apply to what God is currently doing in your life?

6. From what you see in this chapter, what difference was the good news of Jesus actually making in Jerry's life at this time?

Chapter 14: Fruitful Ministry

1. Look again at Ecclesiastes 7:13 and Hebrews 13:5, passages God used in Jerry's life during a trouble-delayed airline trip to Israel. How could these same passages be speaking God's words to you regarding difficulties you're now facing?

   Why did those passages have such power for Jerry at this time?

2. How do you continue seeing God's hand at work in Jerry's experiences during these years?

3. Summarize why Jerry reworded the focus of his teaching from "Grace and Discipline" to "Gospel-Based Transformation."

4. Jerry writes, "Without the gospel there is no grace." What does he mean by that?

Why is it so important that we deeply understand this truth?

After reading Jerry's discussion of this topic, what would you say are the best definitions of the words *grace* and *gospel*?

5. How would you summarize the further truth Jerry was learning about the believer's union with Christ?

Jerry cites 2 Corinthians 5:21 as a strong summation of this truth. What full meaning does this passage have for you?

This truth is further amplified in Paul's words in Philippians 3:9. Look again at this verse; how strongly does it reflect your own heart's desire and expectation?

6. Jerry poses the question, "Where does the gospel fit into a ministry of challenge to the pursuit of holiness?" In your own words, how does he answer this question?

7. "When we go to be with God," Jerry writes, "it is not the awards or recognition we have received, but the lives impacted for Christ that will count when each of us hopes to hear, 'Well done, good and faithful servant' (Matthew 25:21)." How closely and completely does this correspond with your own expectation of reward in eternity?

8. Jerry asks himself why God waited until he was sixty-five to begin this particularly fruitful time of ministry for him in teaching and writing. What answer does he give?

What are your own longings and prayers for fruitfulness and usefulness in the work of God's kingdom during the rest of your time on earth?

9. From what you see in this chapter, what difference was the good news of Jesus actually making in Jerry's life at this time?

Chapter 15: A Time of Reflection

1. What gets your attention most in Jerry's description of these most recent years in his life?

2. How do you most clearly see God's hand at work in Jerry's life during these years?

3. Jerry writes, "We never graduate from God's school of adversity and faith. We will be walking by faith until we die." Do you find this encouraging — or discouraging? And how so?

How can you be best prepared for future times of adversity and faith-testing in your life?

4. In the section of this chapter entitled "Spiritual Lessons," Jerry presents seven lessons that stand out most to him as he looks back on his life. *(They're also reprinted in questions 5–11 below, for your further interaction with them.)*

   Which of these lessons are truths that God has already specifically called your attention to, and how has He done this in your life?

   Which of these lessons are truths that God appears to be currently working on in your life, to deepen your understanding of them?

5. (In the next seven questions, respond fully to each spiritual lesson that Jerry has outlined, as reprinted here.) *"Lesson One: The Bible is meant to be applied to specific life situations. This includes both God's commands to be obeyed and His promises to be relied upon. Here, of course, is where Scripture memorization is so valuable. The Holy Spirit can bring to our minds*

specific Scriptures to apply to specific situations." How fully are you applying both God's commands *and* God's promises to your life?

In your stewardship of the mind God has given you, how regularly and fully are you storing up God's Word inside it, ready for the Holy Spirit to use in His ministry to you?

6. "*Lesson Two: All who trust in Christ as Savior are united to Him in a living way just as the branches are united to the vine (see John 15:15). This means that as we abide in Him — that is, depend on Him in faith — His very life will flow into and through us to enable us to be fruitful both in our own character and our ministry to others.*" How much and how often do you personally sense this "living way" in which the believer is united to Christ?

In John 15:15, what are the most important truths for you in the description Jesus gives here of this living union?

What is the fruitfulness that you believe the Lord wants you to experience?

7. *"Lesson Three: The pursuit of holiness and godly character is neither by self-effort nor simply letting Christ 'live His life through you.' Rather, it does involve our most diligent efforts but with a recognition that we are dependent on the Holy Spirit to enable us and to bless those efforts. I call this 'dependent responsibility.'"* What particular "diligent efforts" is the Lord requiring from you at this time as you live for Him and serve Him in dependence on His Spirit?

From your own experience in living the Christian life, what practical concerns and issues arise as you seek to avoid both a dependence on self-effort and a mere "passive approach"?

How would you define your own responsibility in the pursuit of holiness and godly character?

8. *"Lesson Four: The sudden understanding of the doctrine of election was a watershed event for me that significantly affected my entire Christian life. For example, it was the realization of God's sovereignty in election that led me to study further the sovereignty of God in all of life. It also produced a deep sense of gratitude and, I trust, humility, of realizing salvation was entirely of Him."* In what ways are you most tempted to take personal credit for any aspects of your salvation, rather than giving glory and thanks to God?

How do you see the doctrine of election fitting into the full picture of God's sovereignty over all things?

How can a better understanding of this doctrine of election increase your gratitude toward God?

How can it also deepen your humility?

9. *"Lesson Five: The representative union of Christ and the believer means that all that Christ did in both His perfect obedience and His death for our sins is credited to us. Or to say it another way, because Christ is our representative before the Father, it was just of God to charge our sins to Christ and to credit His righteousness to us. So we*

as believers stand before God perfectly cleansed from both the guilt and defilement of our sin, but also clothed in the perfect righteousness of Christ." How does this teaching increase your interest in the obedient life of Jesus as portrayed in the Gospels?

What do you see as the significant practical aspects of fully understanding this "representative union" between Christ and yourself?

What does the "righteousness" of Christ mean to you? How did Jesus demonstrate and display this righteousness?

10. "*Lesson Six: The gospel is not just for unbelievers in their coming to Christ. Rather all of us who are believers need the gospel every day because we are still practicing sinners. The gospel, embraced every day, helps keep us from self-righteousness because it frees us to see our sin for what it really is. Also, gratitude for what God has done for us in Christ should motivate us to want to pursue godly character and to offer ourselves as living sacrifices to Him.*" How deeply do you actually sense your need for the gospel on a typical day?

How exactly does our embrace of the gospel set us free "to see our sin for what it really is"?

When we don't embrace the gospel, how will we tend to view our sins?

Practically speaking, how does embracing the gospel actually motivate us to pursue godly character and offer ourselves as living sacrifices to God?

11. *"Lesson Seven: We are dependent on the Holy Spirit to apply the life of Christ to our lives. Someone has said (and this is a paraphrase), God the Father purposes, Christ accomplishes what the Father has purposed, and the Holy Spirit applies to our lives what Christ accomplished. To do this, the Spirit works in us directly and He also enables us to work. All the spiritual strength that we need comes to us from Christ through the Holy Spirit."* In what ways do you most clearly see your dependence on the Holy Spirit?

How have you most recently seen the Holy Spirit working in you directly?

How have you most recently seen the Holy Spirit enabling you to work?

What specific freedom do you find in the truth that all the spiritual strength you need comes to you from Christ through the Holy Spirit?

12. In the section of this chapter entitled "The Providence of God," Jerry points his readers to Romans 8:28-29. What do you see as the most important truths in this passage — truths that you need to be fully aware of, grateful for, and committed to?

13. Review the long list of bulleted items here in which Jerry summarizes "significant acts of God's providence in my life," as we've seen them unfold in the earlier chapters.

Which of these events or circumstances are most like situations that have occurred in your own life?

Which of these most clearly communicate to you God's *love* in action?

Which of them stands out most to you as a manifestation of God's *sovereign power*?

Which of them especially show you God's *wisdom* at work?

14. What gets your attention most in this chapter's final section entitled "What About the Future?"

    How do you continue seeing here the hand of God at work in Jerry's life?

15. After reading this book, describe how confidently and gratefully you can make the following declaration about your own life: "God took me by the hand and said, 'Come with Me.'"

More great words from Jerry Bridges!